ENGLISH PAPER PIECING

A Stitch in Time

18 PROJECTS TO INSPIRE
WITH NEEDLE AND THREAD

SHARON BURGESS

Contents

Projects

Tuva Publishing
www.tuvapublishing.com

Address Merkez Mah. Cavusbasi Cad. No:71
Cekmekoy - Istanbul 34782 / Turkey
Tel: +9 0216 642 62 62

English Paper Piecing
"A Stitch In Time"

First Print 2018 / August

All Global Copyrights Belong To
Tuva Tekstil ve Yayıncılık Ltd.

Content Quilting

Editor in Chief Ayhan DEMİRPEHLİVAN
Project Editor Kader DEMİRPEHLİVAN
Designer Sharon BURGESS
Technical Editors Leyla ARAS, Büşra ESER
Graphic Designers Ömer ALP, Abdullah BAYRAKÇI, Zilal ÖNEL
Photograph Tuva Publishing
Photograph Stylist Tuba YÜKSEL
Illustrations Murat Tanhu YILMAZ

ISBN 978-605-9192-46-0

Introduction

Welcome to 'A Stitch in Time', my second book and a place where I am excited to share with you my love of English Paper Piecing in a collection of projects that I hope will 'inspire you with needle and thread'.

I am an 'English born Aussie Girl' and predominately a self-taught quilter. I was born to English Parents in Aldershot in the UK and moved to Australia at a young age with my Mum, Dad and younger brother. I now live in Central Victoria in a beautiful area that is steeped in history from its Gold Rush heritage. We are surrounded by beautiful architecture and a vibrant café life which combines the history of the town beautifully with our modern lifestyle.

Early in my quilting journey I was introduced to English Paper Piecing and with a young family at the time, I fell in love with its portability and I developed a love for hand sewing. I enjoy selecting the perfect fabric, and find great comfort in fussy cutting the different elements of a design, wrapping the fabric around the paper shapes and slowly stitching it all back together again.

As much as I love making larger quilts, I also enjoy the love and details that can be added to a smaller project. Each project within this book has an element of English Paper Piecing, combined with some of my other loves: Vintage Linens, Embroidery, Applique, Patchwork and Quilting.

There is something special about sewing for yourself or sharing a handmade gift with a friend. My hope is that these projects will inspire you to slow down a little in today's fast paced world, to take the time to enjoy the process of the fabric selection, finding the perfect lace or trim and ultimately creating the perfect project. Connect with your hands, slow your mind and enjoy the process.

I hope that you enjoy this slow stitching journey with me and remember to always "Create what YOU love".

Happy stitching,

Sharon

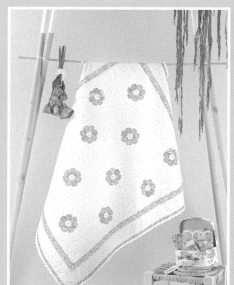

What is English Paper Piecing?

Put simply, English Paper Piecing (commonly referred to as EPP) is a technique used for making quilts by hand where your fabric is basted over a paper template, then the shapes are sewn together to form the quilt or project.

English Paper Piecing is sometimes also known as "Mosaic Patchwork" and when English Paper Piecing is spoken of, hexagon quilts usually come to mind. The hexagon shape has been hugely popular over the centuries and is the shape that has been predominantly used from as far back as the 1700s.

Popular through Europe and specifically England, it became exceptionally fashionable in the United States of America towards late 18th Century. when anything English was considered highly fashionable.

One of the most popular and most recognizable English Paper Piecing patterns was and still is, the "Grandmother's Flower Garden". It is based around seven simple hexagons sewn together to form a flower shape. It could be used to create a simple block, or with more sewn together, it could form an entire quilt. With the onset of the Great Depression in the USA in the 1930s, this quilt pattern could easily be created with leftover fabric scraps, with the papers being recycled from documents and books.

PAPERS AND TEMPLATES

Paper shapes are the backbone of English Paper Piecing projects, and a wide variety of pre-cut paper pieces can be purchased to create almost anything. As the pre-cut paper pieces are professionally die-cut, accuracy is assured. This is critical for EPP.

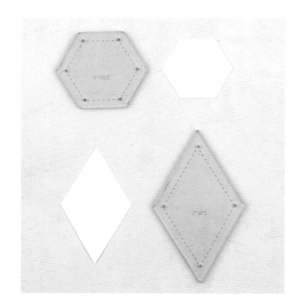

You can cut your own template shapes, but care needs to be taken to ensure accuracy.

There are some shapes used in these patterns that are not readily available. You will see these shapes marked with an * on them - see Templates (pages 142-159).

For shapes that are not available in your local quilt shop, you will need to transfer the shape onto cardstock/thick paper (I use a 160gsm cardstock) and then cut them yourself. Please see 'A quick word on custom shapes' on page 16.

Acrylic templates are used to assist you in cutting and tracing the required shape onto your fabric. They come complete with a seam allowance for basting to your paper pieces. They are clear to allow you to see what you are cutting, essential when fussy cutting. They can be commonly purchased with a ¼" or ⅜" seam allowance.

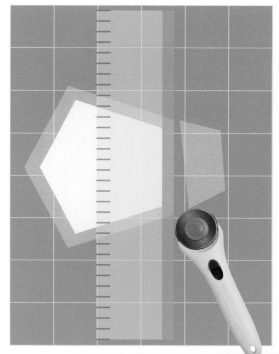

TIP: Making Your Own Template
Lay a paper shape onto some template plastic and carefully, with a rotary cutter and an add-a-quarter ruler cut the template plastic ¼" bigger than your shape. A plastic template is easier to mark reference points for fussy cutting with a pencil and the marks simply erase off.

MY ESSENTIAL ENGLISH PAPER PIECING TOOLS

Having the right tools on hand will make your English Paper Piecing journey a more enjoyable one.
All the items I have here can be found in your local patchwork shop or easily online.

- Size 10 or 11 Milliner's needles (also known as straw needles)
- Thread
- Glue pen and refills
- Rotary cutters - both 60mm and 28mm
- Scissors
- Rotating cutting mat
- Cutting mat
- Sandpaper board
- Quilting clips

- Pencil
- Appliqué glue
- Patchwork ruler
- Fussy Cutting Mirror
- Add-a-quarter-ruler
- Seam ripper
- ¼" masking tape
- 'Flatter' by SOAK

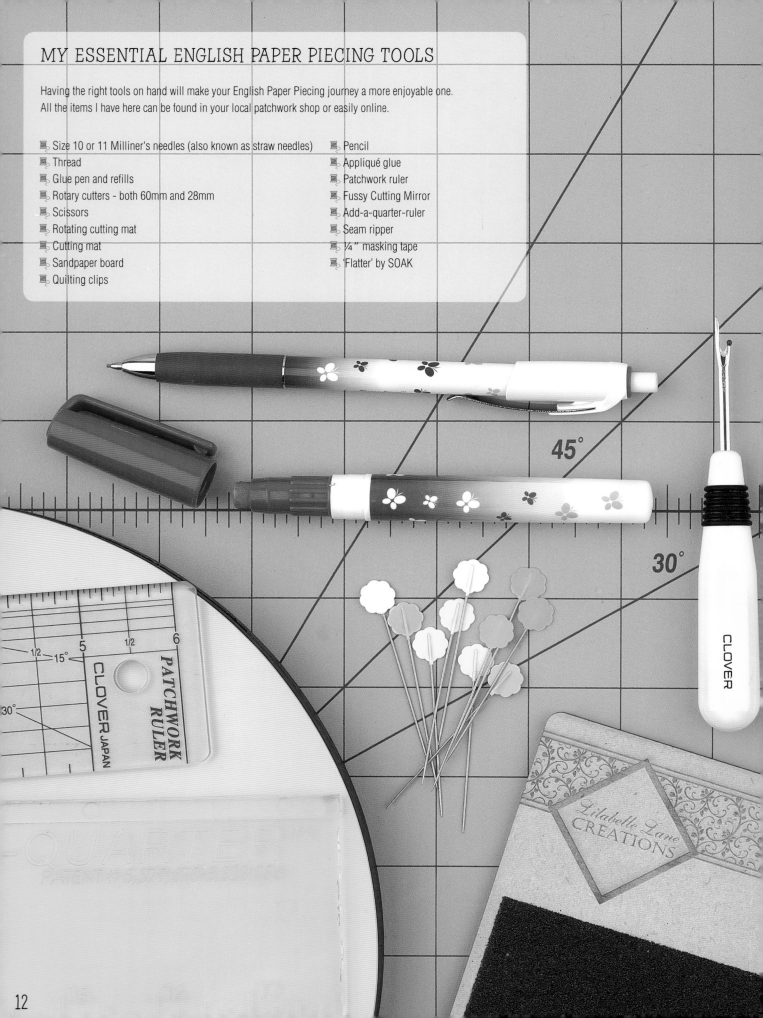

Fussy Cutting Mirror

create
what YOU love

CLOVER CUTTING MAT

13

My Essential Tools

Having the right tools on hand will make your Sewing and English Paper Piecing journey a more enjoyable one. If you can, it is worth investing in quality tools. Everything I use can be found in quality quilt and craft shops.

▶ MY SEWING MACHINE

I use a Brother Innov-is VQ3000. It has a nice wide throat space for quilting, a large table work area and a great variety of feet. My most commonly used foot is the ¼″ foot - great for accuracy in achieving a consistent ¼″ seam allowance.

▶ THREAD

In my Sewing Machine, I choose to use Aurifil 50wt. For my English Paper Piecing, I use Superior Bottom Line Thread 60wt. For my embroidery, I choose DMC Floss and Perle Cotton No 8 for hand quilting.

▶ NEEDLES

Everyone has their favorite. Size 10 and 11 Milliners Needles (also known as Straw needles) are mine. Teaming a quality needle with quality thread will allow you to achieve beautiful invisible stitches.

▶ SEAM RIPPER

A nice sharp seam ripper is essential to help with any reverse sewing. Investing in a quality one will save you so much time and will provide a better result when unpicking a seam.

▶ ROTARY CUTTERS AND SCISSORS

I use my 60mm Rotary Cutter when cutting out for a larger project or quilt and my smaller 28mm Rotary cutter when cutting around an English Paper Piecing Template. I also have my go-to Fabric Sheers, multiple comfortable pairs of small embroidery scissors for cutting my thread and then my older scissors for cutting paper.

▶ CUTTING MACHINE

I also have a Brother Scan N Cut (CM900) that I use to cut a lot of my own EPP papers. I use a 160gsm to 220gsm cardstock for my papers. All the shapes used in this book can be copied and scanned into a Scan N Cut.

▶ CUTTING MATS

I use a large self-healing cutting mat as well as Rotating Cutting mat for smaller pieces. The Rotating cutting mat is great for trimming Half Square triangles and when basting EPP Shapes. The Rotating Mat is a great tool to help you achieve nice smooth curved surfaces when basting your papers.

▶ PATCHWORK RULERS

I have various sizes to help me with my day to day patchwork. It is important to buy rulers that have thin lines marked on them to help you maintain to your accuracy. I also cannot go past my Add a Quarter Ruler. It is a great tool to help when making your own templates and anywhere that you need to add a ¼″ seam allowance, also great for foundation piecing.

▶ GLUE PEN AND REFILLS

The Sewline Glue Pens and refills are a great alternative to thread basting your EPP.

▶ SANDPAPER BOARD

A Sandpaper board helps to eliminate movement when you place your fabric on it and then trace around your English Paper Piecing Shapes.

▶ FUSSY CUTTING MIRROR

With the investment of a Fussy Cutting mirror you will be able to see all your options within your pattern repeats and how you can use these repeats to create new and exciting patterns before you start to cut your fabrics.

▶ QUILTING CLIPS

These are great to hold your pieces together as you stitch and to help prevent movement. They can help you reduce strain on your hand from holding your pieces too tight. They are also great for holding groups of prepared EPP Shapes / pieces together for when you are stitching on the go. I also use them for holding my binding down on projects as I stitch.

APPLIQUE GLUE

Allows you to position your appliqued shapes to another piece of fabric. It is great for allowing you to prepare your hand stitching work so that you can take it with you on the go and not need to worry about any pins.

MASKING TAPE

I use ¼" Masking Tape to help keep my hand quilting lines straight. Line the tape along where you want to hand quilt and follow the edge so that your quilting lines stay nice and straight. The tape can then be reused and moved to your next position.

FLATTER BY SOAK

I prefer to use Flatter by Soak on all my sewing. It is a starch-free smoothing agent that leaves my sewing 'sleek, soft and static free'.

PENCILS AND MARKERS

I have three essentials. First is a re-fillable clutch pencil for tracing around my EPP Templates onto my fabric. The Clutch Pencil allows a constant thin line with no need to sharpen. A Millennium Pen in a Brown with a tip size of 03 to transfer Embroidery designs onto my fabric before stitching. Lastly, a water-soluble pen for marking quilting lines on my projects or marking where clasps etc. are to be placed.

EMBELLISHMENTS

In my studio I have a box that holds my collection of trims, laces, leather tags, buttons, zipper pulls and ribbons. These are all things that I gather in my travels knowing that one day they will be there when I need that perfect embellishment for a special project.

PELLON FUSIBLE FLEECE

Is a light weight, thin fusible batting/wadding that can be used behind stitcheries to stop shadowing or distortions. I also like to use it in my smaller projects, especially those that I am applying some hand quilting detail to. I also use it to back my English Paper Pieced Panels made from such fabrics as Lawns and Vintage Linens.

GLOSSARY OF TERMS

EPP – English Paper Piecing
RST – Right Sides Together
WOF –Width of Fabric
HST – Half Square Triangle

All seams are ¼" unless otherwise stated.
All Embroidery is stitched in two strands of DMC Floss unless otherwise stated.

Techniques

►ENGLISH PAPER PIECING

English Paper Piecing is the technique of wrapping fabric around a pre-cut paper shape to stabilize it and form shapes. The fabric is basted to the shape and sewn together by hand. You can thread baste or glue baste. I choose to glue baste.

Pre-cut paper pieces are available in various sizes to suit your needs. Each project within this book will require English Paper Piecing papers, most of which can be purchased with the coordinating Perspex template at your Local Quilt Shop or in online stores. Alternatively, these shapes can also be made at home by copying the shapes from the template pages onto 160 - 220gsm card and then cut the shapes out by hand. You can also use one of the many cutting machines that are on the market. I use my "Brother Scan N Cut" machine for cutting most of my EPP Shapes.

►TEMPLATES

Each English Paper piecing paper shape can be purchased with the coordinating Perspex template. The templates include the seam allowance needed for your fabric. Most

templates have either a ¼" or 3/8" seam allowance. Which one you use is purely a personal preference. I choose to use the templates with the ¼" seam allowance. You only need to purchase the Perspex templates once. Most templates will also have holes in them. These are usually located at the corners or points, and correspond with where the papers will sit on the fabric. These holes are used to mark reference points onto your fabric so that you can position your papers accurately which is important when fussy cutting.

You may also choose to make your own templates.

►A QUICK WORD ON CUSTOM SHAPES

Some of the projects included in this book use 'custom shapes'. These custom shapes have been marked with a * on the template pages. These shapes are not commercially available. For your convenience please visit www.lilabellelanecreations.com/AStitchInTime/templates to download the complimentary templates. This link is case sensitive and needs to be entered into your Web Browser's Address bar, not the Internet search function.

CREATING A TEMPLATE

Creating a template to coordinate with your papers is easy and quick. You will require a piece of template plastic slightly larger than your paper shape and one of your paper shapes.

1 Using a piece of tape rolled over with the sticky side facing out, stick the paper shape to the template plastic ensuring there is at least a ¼" gap all around.

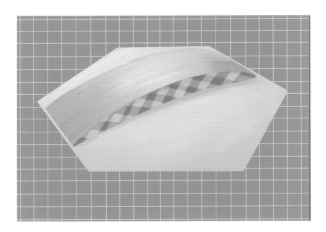

2 Take an Add a Quarter ruler and use the little lip edge to rest against the paper and with your rotary cutter, carefully cut the template plastic on all edges. This will give you your template.

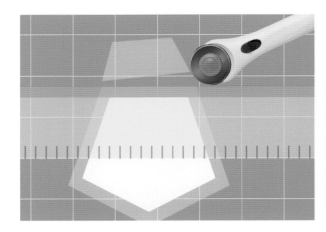

3 To mark the paper size onto your template, take a permanent marker and draw half over the edge of the paper, half over the template plastic all the way around, leaving a nice sharp inside line marking the papers edge. Remove the paper and tape and your template is ready to use.

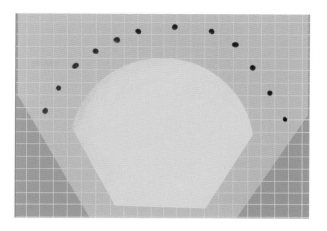

Trace around the paper with the marker as per Step 3 and your template is ready to use.

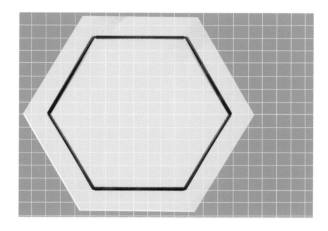

To make a template that has a curved side the process is the same but this time trim the straight edges and then mark reference points around the curve with the ruler and marker. Cut along the curve with old scissors.

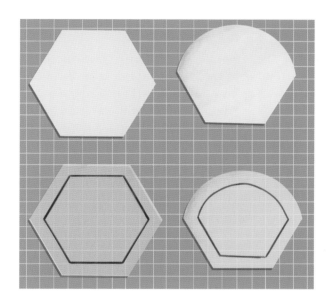

CUTTING YOUR EPP SHAPES FROM FABRIC / FUSSY CUTTING

English Paper Piecing allows you the opportunity to fussy cut your fabrics. There are two types of fussy cutting. The first is when you are highlighting an element of a fabric. An example of this is used in the Octagons of the "Little Miss Sweetness Bag".

Kaleidoscope fussy cutting can achieve some great results and allow you to add that extra flair to your project. By using a Fussy Cutting mirror and placing it over your fabrics you will be able to see what effect you can achieve before you cut into your fabrics. The best kaleidoscope fussy cutting is achieved from designs or an element of a design that are symmetrical which simply means one side is the exact mirror image to the other.

FUSSY CUTTING

If you choose to fussy cut your fabrics for a project, you can simply lay your template over the section of the fabric that you wish to highlight and with a pencil trace around the shape. I always trace on the wrong side of the fabric as this eliminates the need to remove the pencil markings from the right side of your fabric if you make a tracing error.

Keep a fussy cutting mirror handy so that you can explore all the fussy cutting opportunities before making the final decision on where to cut.

With pointed end scissors, snip in and cut the shape out along the drawn line. I prefer this method as opposed to using your rotary cutter as the rotary cutter will cut slightly into the remaining fabric and could potentially limit a future fussy cutting opportunity.

ALWAYS check that you have the required number of repeats before cutting into your fabrics.

When you are placing a template over a fabric ready to fussy cut/trace have a closer look at where you have the template positioned. Look for any 'reference points' in the pattern that will assist you with placing that template in the same position on each pattern repeat. Sometimes by moving your template over a little the fussy cutting can become easier to repeat. A template made from template plastic is also a great tool for patterns that have no clear 'reference points'. Using a pencil, trace any element of the design as reference points onto the template plastic and use that to line up the pattern repeat.

For both examples, I have rested the template on points that will be easy to repeat. The first has the template resting at the bottom of the over the Teal feature with the bottom hole in the template resting in the center of the print. The second picture shows the top hole of the template aligned with the center of the green flower.

STRIP CUTTING

If you are not fussy cutting your fabrics, you can strip cut your fabrics. Strip cutting is a fast way to cut the fabric ready for English Paper Piecing.

Strip cutting is as simple as measuring the height of your template, remembering that a template includes your seam allowance and a paper does not, and cutting strips of fabric to this height with your patchwork ruler and rotary cutter. If you are a confident quilter and have a sharp blade in your rotary cutter, you can layer multiple strips of fabric and then use your Perspex template and your rotary cutter to cut your shapes.

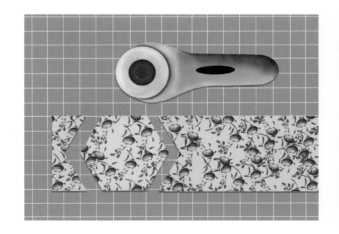

HOW ARE THE SHAPES MEASURED?

Geometric shapes are measured by the length of one of the equal sides. You can see that this hexagon has a 1″ side, therefore it is referred to as a 1″ Hexagon.

Here are a few other examples.

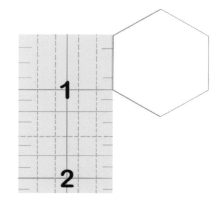

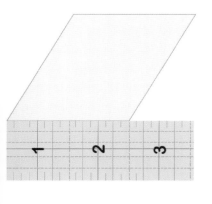

2.5″ Six Pointed Star

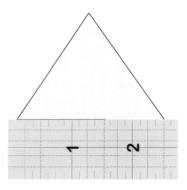

2.5″ Equilateral Triangle

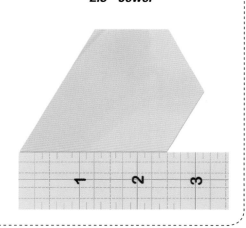

2.5″ Jewel

Hexagon Flower petals take their measurement from the straight edge that sews to the center hexagon. Here an example of a 1″ Hexagon Flower Petal.

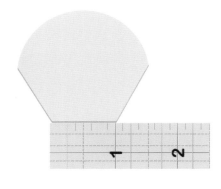

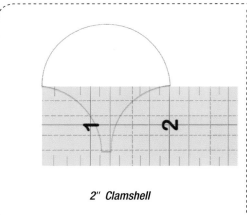

2″ Clamshell

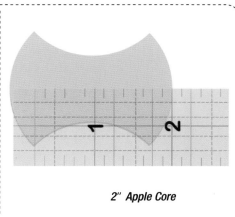

2″ Apple Core

Curved paper pieces are measured across the diameter.

Getting Started

Glue Basting is a simple and time effective way to prepare your papers and fabrics for stitching. A good habit to develop early on is to always baste your papers in the same direction regardless of the shape. This becomes essential when you are using diamonds/stars and triangles as it means your tails will all nest in, lay flat and spiral around at their meeting point at the back. This will create a neater finish and a flatter centre to your work.

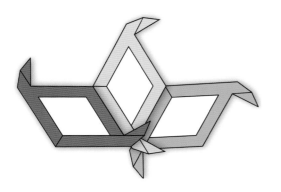

When you come to sew your shapes together fold any little tails out of the way, do not stitch them down or into your work.

When glue basting, it is important to remember that "less is more" with the glue and this will come with practice over time.

TIP: In a warmer climate, you can store your Glue Pen and refills in a refrigerator, in an air tight container or place your glue pen and refills in the refrigerator a half hour before use to firm up the glue and prevent excess usage.

▶ How to Glue Baste Your Papers

1 Lay your fabrics right side down, place your paper on top and centre it in the middle of the fabric.

2 Holding your Glue Pen on an angle, just like you hold a pen, glide it across the paper slightly away from the edge.

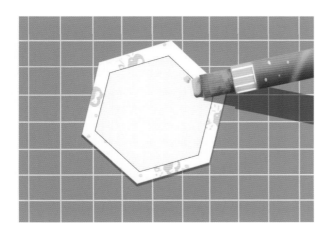

3 Fold over the fabric and press down. Continue to the next side and repeat. Ensure that your points are nice and sharp. Repeat for all the sides of your shape.

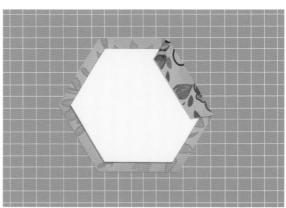

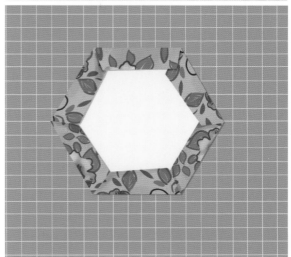

This process is the same for all straight sided shapes.

Preparing Shapes with Curves

Clamshells

When preparing Clam Shells, you only need to baste the convex curve.

1 Lay your fabric right side facing down and place your paper on top, centring it. Holding your Glue Pen on an angle glide it across the curve of the paper slightly away from the edge.

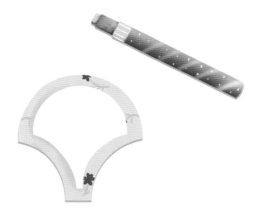

2 At the starting point, ensure that you pull the fabric over so that you have a nice firm fold and your fabric sits vertical.

3 Fold your fabrics over the curve forming little pleats as you go. The pleats will be at the back of your shape and the front should be nice and smooth. If you do this step on a rotating mat, turning the mat and not the shape, you can achieve a smoother curve quickly as you are not moving the paper and fabric, only the rotating mat.

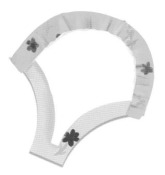

4 At your ending point, ensure that the fabric is again pressed over so that you have a nice firm fold and your fabric sits vertical.

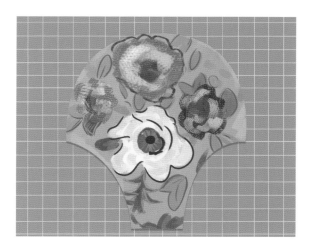

►Hexagon Flower Petals

When preparing a Flower petal shape you use the combined technique for both a standard shape and a curve.

1 Lay your fabric right side facing down and centre your paper on top.

2 Holding your Glue Pen on an angle, just like you hold a pen, glide it across the paper slightly away from the edge.

3 Fold the fabric over the straight edge and press down firmly on the glue.

4 Glide your glue pen across the curve of the paper slightly away from the edge.

5 Fold your fabrics over the curve forming little pleats at the back as you go, the fabric at the front of the shape should be nice and smooth.

6 Continue to glue around the remainder of the shape, folding the fabric over the paper, pressing firmly onto the glue and creating nice points at the corners as you go.

►Let's Talk Thread

For all my English Paper Piecing, I personally choose to use "Superior Threads – The Bottom Line" in a 60wt. It is a polyester thread. Traditionally if you are working with cotton fabric you would use a cotton thread but with English Paper Piecing it is important to realise that every time you make a stitch, your thread has the potential to rub against the paper template. When using a cotton thread, it can fray and snap. I have found I that the Superior Thread does not and works best for me.

The Superior Thread is available in 1,420 yard spools, pre-wound onto bobbins which can be purchased individually or in packs and as a SuperBOB Donut which has 35 different colored bobbins stored in a red bobbin saver.

▸Joining the Pieces – Straight Edged Shapes

1 Thread your needle with a coordinated thread and tie a knot in one end.

2 Place two shapes right side together. Slide your needle up under the fabric at the start point and pull through to bury your knot.

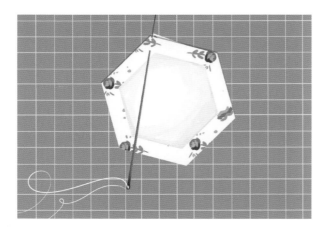

3 At the start point of your seam, slide the needle through both pieces of fabric, ensuring that you only catch a couple of threads and not the paper and do your first stitch.

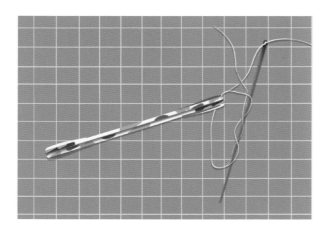

4 Secure your stitch on top of where you have just taken your first stitch. I secure my stitches by leaving a small loop in my thread and wrapping the needle through the loop twice and pulling through.

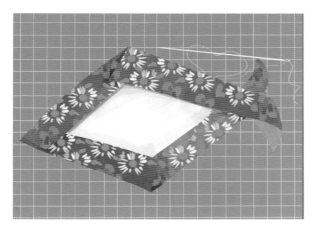

5 Using a Whip stitch (refer to "Hand and Embroidery Stitches" in the Techniques section), stitch along the edge of your shapes making small stitches, securing your thread at the end. Remember with your Whip Stitch to stitch the most direct path i.e. directly across the two pieces, not on an angle.

6 Open and then proceed to join in your next piece. There is no right or wrong way in which order to sew hexagons together and because you have not placed the glue right to the edge of your papers you should be able to carry your thread under the fabric to your next spot to start stitching therefore saving you from knotting off your work, cutting your thread and restarting.

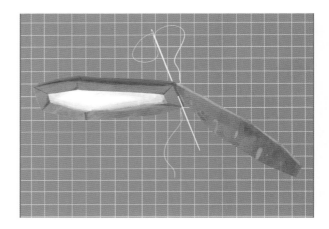

Here is an example of how you might sew a hexagon flower together.

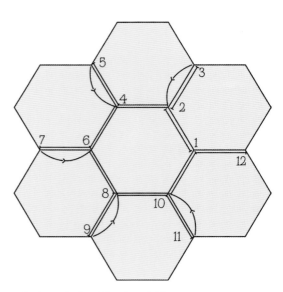

Sew from point 1 to point 2 and then to point 3.
Take your needle under the fabric back to point 2 then sew from point 2 to 4 and on to 5.
Take your needle under the fabric back to point 4 then sew from point 4 to 6 and on to 7.
Take your needle under the fabric back to point 6 then sew from point 6 to 8 and on to 9.
Take your needle under the fabric back to point 8 then sew from point 8 to 10 and on to 11.
Take your needle under the fabric back to point 10 then sew from point 10 to 1 and on to 12 and you have worked your way around a hexagon flower.

7 Before removing any papers, give your work a gentle press on a warm setting. To remove the papers just peel back the seam allowance at the back and pull the papers out. You should only have to peel back one or two sides to slide your finger in to pull the paper out. If you are having trouble removing your papers you may have used too much glue. Gently press with a steam iron to soften the glue and continue to remove the papers. Papers can also be removed from a project as it grows. You only need to leave the papers in the outer most edge of your work.

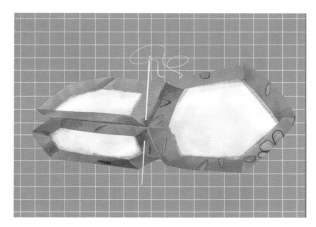

TIP: Don't be scared to fold your papers to bring your seams together or to make it easier to hold your work in your hand. Remember that you only need to leave the papers in the outer most edge of your work.

Diamonds and Jewels

When joining diamonds, jewels or any shape where multiple points all meet, you need to first join your pieces in sections: - half or quarter units and then join those sections together to form the bigger unit.

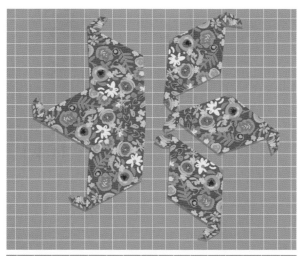

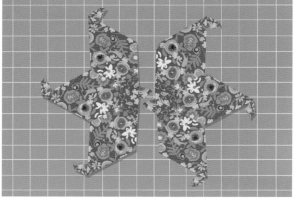

For example, with 6 Pointed Diamonds or Jewels, sew two sections of three and then sew those two sections together, from one side right through the middle to the other side folding the excess 'tail' fabric out of the way as you sew across. This will stop any holes forming at the meeting point of all your points and allow you a better result and neater finish of where those points do meet.

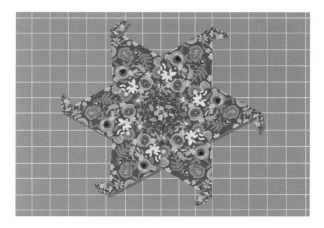

If sewing an 8 (pictured below) or 10 pointed star, then the process is the same, two halves of 4 or 5 and then sew the two halves together. The picture below also shows you how breaking a project up into smaller sections makes it easier to assemble.

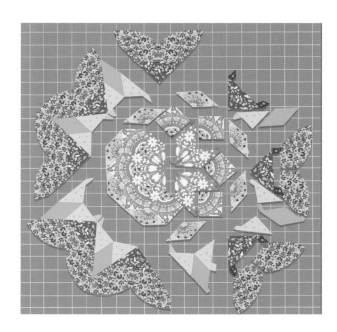

Any larger unit can be broken down into smaller units to make construction easier.

Once you have finished a section give it a gentle press with a warm iron before removing any papers. This helps give your seams a nice neat and flat finish.

Joining the Pieces - Clamshells

Joining your clamshells are a little different to the normal EPP process. Prepare your Clamshell papers and fabric as per the Glue Basting Curves instructions. Lay your prepared Clamshells out in a pleasing manner.

Clamshells are first joined together in rows and then appliqued togther.

To join your rows:

1 Thread your needle with a coordinated thread and tie a knot in one end.

2 Face two Clamshells right sides together and "kiss the points" by aligning the points at the start of the curve. Make your first stitch right at the position where the papers align.

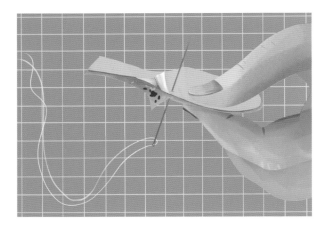

3 Make a couple of stitches on top of each other and then secure your stitch. Cut your thread and repeat the process to make a row of your desired number of clamshells. Repeat for required number of rows.

4 To begin to sew your rows together get a piece of fabric a little longer than the panel you plan to make and with your iron, press a fold line a minimum of half the diameter of your clamshell. For example, if you are working with a 2" clamshell then fold and press a line approximately 1" along the bottom with your iron. A 3" clamshell would require a minimum of a 1.5" fold line, a 4" clamshell would require 2" and so on.

5 Using your applique glue, place three or four small dots of glue on the seam allowance on the back of each clamshell. Flip over and align the top curve of the clamshell on the fold line. Allow the glue to dry naturally. Alternatively, do this step at your ironing board so that you can give everything a quick iron once glued into position to help set the glue faster.

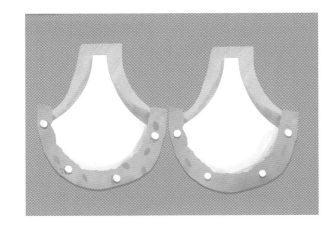

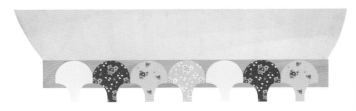

6 Applique your clamshells onto the fabric using a Blind Stitch. Stitch around the first curve to where you "kissed your points", then go up and over your next curve and continue until the row is completed. See "Blind Stitch" instructions in the "Hand and Embroidery Stitches" in the Techniques section.

7 To remove your papers, you need to gently pull them out in a curved motion in line with the curve of the Clamshell. If you are having trouble removing your papers you may have used too much glue. If this is the case, take your panel to your iron and on a warm steam setting, press your work. This will soften the glue and help you remove your papers.

8 Line up your next prepared row, flip it to the wrong side and apply three or four dots of applique glue to the seam allowance on the back of each clamshell (As per step 5).

9 Flip over onto your previous row. This time you are aligning the top middle of the Clamshell curve to the spot where you "kissed your points". Applique this row on as per step 6.

For further rows repeat from Steps 6 – 9.

My Preferred Applique Method

There are many ways to applique a shape to a background. My preferred Applique method when working with EPP involves leaving in the outer most papers in your work. This helps with achieving a nice curved edge to your work as your papers are still in place and the folds over the papers stay nice and crisp. If you remove the papers you may have to re-iron your work and this can cause you to lose the straight edge or the curve that was there whilst the papers were in place.

1 Once your English Paper Pieced panel / flower or shape is completed remove all the papers except those on the outer most edge of all the sides that will be appliqued.

2 Gently press your work with a warm iron.

3 Prepare the background fabric as per the pattern.

4 Flip the English Paper Pieced panel so the wrong side is facing up and apply small dots of Applique glue to the seam allowance on the outer edge of your work. DO NOT apply glue to the inside seams.

5 Flip the English Paper Pieced panel back over and position it onto the background and press.

6 When the glue is dry, Applique the shape into place using a blind stitch. See 'Hand and Embroidery Stitches' in the Techniques section.

7 Turn the panel over so that you have the back of the work facing you and CAREFULLY with a sharp pair of scissors, cut away the background fabric that is behind the English Paper Pieced panel ensuring that you are at least ¼" inside the sewn line. This will expose the back of your English Paper Pieced Panel and the remaining papers. If needed, cut slits into the petals or point like in the examples shown to help you remove the papers easier.

8 Gently press your work and continue as per the pattern instructions.

Vintage Linens

My love of vintage linens began when my own girls were little. I started visiting Thrift shops to find little trinkets and treasures for my girl's rooms. Crystal plates for their earrings, glasses for their hair accessories. When I began my own quilting journey I fully began to appreciate the time and love that was in every handmade item. I found myself bringing home vintage doilies, table runners, pillow cases etc. and tucking them away for safe keeping. Just knowing that someone had spent many hours creating these beauties and now they were left in a thrift shop, I could not bring myself to leave them there unloved.

Vintage cottons, bed linens, table cloths and more were once considered to be an important part of a woman's personal belongings. The embroidery and lace tatting could potentially take the maker hundreds of hours to complete. Many of these items would have been passed down through families, sometimes sold to new owners to enjoy, others taken to thrift shops, maybe because the owner had passed or the new owner could not see past a stain or hole. Repurposing a vintage linen that may have a stain or be worn in a spot gives it new life, another chance to be enjoyed and loved.

Finding the perfect linen to include in a project can be satisfying and extremely difficult at the same time. Sometimes making that first cut can be the hardest. For me it can be easier if the linen has a stain that I have unable to remove or a section of the embroidery is damaged.

When starting a project, it can be easier to pick the piece/s of vintage treasures that you wish to include first and then pick your fabrics and colours.

The colour pallet for the 'Stitch in Time Project Folder' was based around the vintage linens I had chosen to include.

A vintage linen can be included in almost any patchwork project with a little care. If the linen is thin it may be best to back it with Pellon, a fusible fleece or similar product.

Linens that have a pretty lace edge are also fun to include and to achieve this effect here is quick and easy.

1   Cut the linen out larger than you need.

2   Position a complimenting piece of fabric under the lace edge and pin into place. Ensure that you have the lace edge at least ½" over the complimenting fabric. The excess behind the linen will be trimmed away later.

3   With a sewing machine, sew along the edge where the vintage linen meets the lace. Try to pick a spot where the stitches will blend.

4   Place a template over the section you wish to use and cut - or – with a rotary cutter and patchwork ruler trim the completed piece to size.

5   On the back of the cut block, remove the excess fabric. If the edge is straight you can fold back the fabric, right sides facing and trim. If the edge is curved, it is best to use your scissors to trim away any excess.

6   Add your trimmed block to your project and enjoy.

Hand and Embroidery Stitches

▶ BACK STITCH

Back Stitch is quick and easy embroidery stitch and a great choice if you are looking for a solid line. When working this stitch try to keep your stitches at an even, consistent length. Bring your thread up from behind your work at point 1 and take it backwards and down through your fabric at point 2. Then bring it back up, one stitch length in front (this will be point 3) and then down again at point 1. Continue this pattern, remembering to keep your stitches of a consistent length.

▶ BLANKET STITCH

Knot one end of your thread and bring your needle up from the back of your work approximately ¼″ down from the edge. Take the thread around to the back of the fabric and bring it up to the front again in the same place. Bring the needle through the stitched loop, from left to right and pull the thread straight up to tighten the stitch. Take another stitch approximately ¼″ to the left (point 2). Pull the thread almost all the way through, leaving a loop. Bring the needle through the loop from the back (point 3) before gently pulling it tight. Repeat these steps to continue.

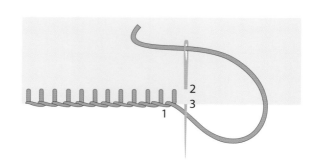

▶ BLIND STITCH

The most commonly used stitch for Appliquéing onto a background.
Knot the end of a single thread and bring your needle up through the underneath of your background fabric barely piercing the edge of the piece you are appliqueing. Place the needle back into the background fabric directly opposite where you came out and bring the needle back up through all the fabrics about 1/16″ on from the last stitch. Continue all the way around your applique piece. Take the needle and thread to the back of your work and knot to finish.

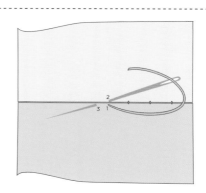

▶ FRENCH KNOT

Bring your needle up from the back. Point the needle downward near where you have just come through and wrap the thread around the needle two times. Position the tip of the needle a couple of threads over from when you came out and pull the needle and thread through the double wrap and back down through the fabric. Anchor your thread on the back.

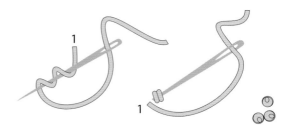

▶ LAZY DAISY STITCH

Bring your needle up from the back at point 1 then push it down right next to 1 and bring it back up at 2, looping the thread under the needle. To anchor your stitch, push the needle back down on the other side of the loop. Repeat for your desired number of petals. When transferring a lazy daisy stitch from an embroidery design, only transfer the dots, not the petal lines. Tip: If you want your petals to be nice, soft and rounded, do not pull your thread too tight.

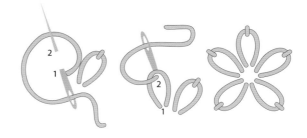

LONG AND SHORT STITCH

This is a textured version of a Satin Stitch and is great to use as a filler for flower petals. Work the first row of stitches inwards along and edge alternating from long to short stitches. Continue to work the next rows, alternating from long to short stitches until you have filled in your desired space. Another alternative is to stitch your second and consecutive rows of long and short stitch so that the top of each stitch goes into the row above. The stitches will be going on a slight angle.

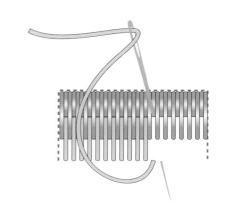

RUNNING STITCH

Running Stitch would be one of the commonly used Embroidery stitches. Knot the end of your thread and bring your needle up at 1, down at 2, up at three and down at four. With this stitch, you need to try and keep your stitches are regular intervals and keep and even tension to avoid your stitches from puckering. I also like use a ¼" Quilters masking tape to help keep my lines straight on my work.

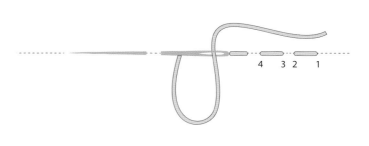

SATIN STITCH

Satin stitch is made up of straight stitches worked close together. Simply sew from point 1 to point 2 and repeat until the desired space is filled.

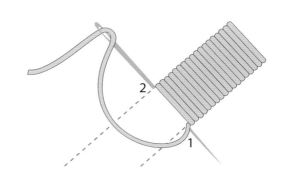

SPLIT STITCH

Bring your needle up from the back of your work to the front and then down a short distance to the right. Bring the needle and thread up through the middle of the stitch you just made, splitting the stitch. Continue to work your line, just like a backstitch but continuing to come up through the previous stitch splitting the thread in the centre to form nice even stitches.

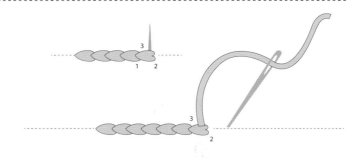

WHIP STITCH

Knot one end of your single thread. Push your needle and thread through both layers of fabric only taking a few threads from both. Take the needle to the back and bring it back through both layers again. Ensure that your stitches are taking the shortest path by coming straight through your fabrics, not on an angle.

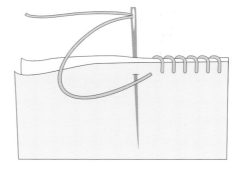

29

Patchwork and Quilting

The projects in this book assume that you have a basic knowledge of patchwork and quilting. If you are new to patchwork I recommend taking a beginner's course at your Local Quilt shop or looking online for some beginner friendly video tutorials. Classes at your local Quilt shop are also a great way to meet like-minded people in your area.

A few beginner tips to help you on your way.

🧵 If your sewing machine did not come with a ¼" foot I would strongly suggest sourcing one as this will help you maintain a consistent ¼" seam. A walking foot is also great to use when you are quilting the three layers of a quilt or smaller project together.

🧵 When quilting and working with quilt blocks, it is important to understand that we only apply our iron vertically, we are not ironing our blocks or quilt tops sideways as this can stretch our fabric, distort our blocks and interfere with block accuracy.

🧵 When you have made a block, check it to ensure it finishes at the correct size. Picking up on an error early, especially when making a larger quilt, can save a lot of frustration later as little inaccuracies can add up, causing bigger problems as your project grows.

🧵 Change the blades of your rotary cutter on a regular basis.

🧵 Most importantly, have fun, learn from your mistakes and "Create what YOU love".

▶ QUILT SANDWICH

A quilt sandwich is the formation of the three layers of a quilt: - the backing, the batting/wadding and the quilt top. To make a quilt sandwich lay your backing fabric right sides down and lay your batting on top. Lay your quilt top on the batting, right side facing up. Baste the layers together with either basting spray (follow the instructions on the can), curved quilting pins.

or hand baste with thread. Check to make sure that you have no large wrinkles or gathers in your backing before quilting.

When it comes to quilting your project, you have a few options:

▶ HAND QUILTING

Hand quilting adds a special touch to any project. It can take a little longer to finish your project but the effect is worth it when it is all done. Basically, hand quilting is simply a running stitch done by hand. I choose to use 2 or 3 strands of coordinating DMC Embroidery floss for smaller projects or DMC Perle Cotton No 8 for larger projects.

When you hand quilt, you need to bury your knots as you go into the batting of your project. To do this, take your threaded needle up through your project from the back and give the thread a gentle tug so that the knot goes through the backing fabric and bury into the batting of your project. If a little hole is left in the backing fabric, 'scratch' it with your finger to ease the fabric fibres back into place. You can then start to quilt your project with nice even stitches.

To help you achieve straight quilting lines whilst hand quilting, you can use a water erasable pen and mark your quilting lines or, and this is my preferred method, place some ¼" quilters tape along where you wish to quilt and follow your needle and thread along the edge of the tape. You can reposition your tape and continue quilting.

You can also use templates, handmade or purchased to hand quilt different designs onto your projects.

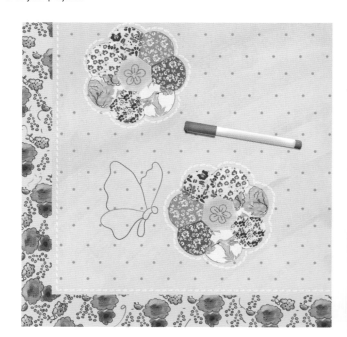

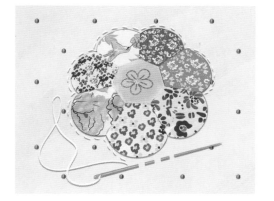

STRAIGHT LINE QUILTING

Straight line quilting with your domestic sewing machine would have to be one of the simplest forms of quilting, which is best done with a walking foot on your machine. You can choose to 'stitch in the ditch' which is when your quilting lines lay in the seams of your patchwork blocks or you can choose to quilt diagonal, horizontal or vertical lines at either regular or irregular intervals depending on the effect you are after. Another popular variation to straight line quilting is when you set your machine up to do a 'serpentine stitch', which is like a zig zag but with more of a wave effect and you quilt these lines either horizontal or vertically across your project.

FREE MOTION QUILTING

Free motion quilting can also be performed on your domestic sewing machine. You need to lower your feed dogs on your machine, this allows your quilt to side freely, and use an open toed quilting / darning foot. Free motion quilting can be as elaborate as you like with intricate designs like feathers or pebbles to a simple stipple.

▶ PROFESSIONAL LONG ARM QUILTING

If you have a larger quilt that you do not want to quilt yourself you can send it out to be professional long arm quilted. With this option, you have the choice of an edge to edge design or you can go for a custom design in consultation with the quilter. I personally send all my large quits out to be professionally quilted as I love the look that is achieved.

"Flourish Quilt" by Lilabelle Lane Creations
Long arm quilted by Linda at Ladybug Quilting, Australia

►BINDING

For larger projects like quilts I like to cut my binding strips at 2.5". For smaller projects where I am using Pellon instead of a higher loft quilt batting I prefer to cut my binding strips at 2". When calculating the amount of binding required remember to allow extra to cover the seam allowance when joining your strips and the overlap when joining the seam on your project. I always make more than required so that I have a nice scrappy stash of binding for when the right project comes along.

1 With your Rotary cutter and self-healing cutting mat, cut the required number of strips from your fabric.

2 Lay your fabrics right sides together and perpendicular to each other, lining up the edges. Draw a 45-degree line and sew along this line with your machine. Trim ¼" away from the sewn line. Continue until all your strips are joined.

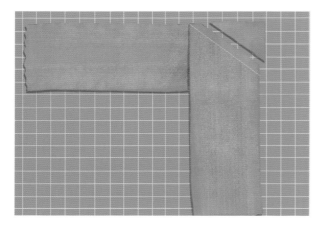

3 Press your seam open. Repeat to make the required amount of binding.

4 Fold in half lengthways, wrong side together and press.

5 At the start of your binding you need to create a point so open the binding and fold down the point and press with your iron. Fold the binding back and press again.

Ensure that your project or quilt has been squared up and then attach your binding.

6 Start at the middle of one edge laying your binding on the right side of your quilt. I usually start at the bottom but on smaller projects start at the most inconspicuous place. Leave 5" of binding not stitched down. Stitch with the raw edges of the binding to the raw edge of the quilt. Stitch through all the layers, ensuring that you back stitch at the start.

7 When you approach the corner, stop ¼" from the end. Lift your presser foot and pull quilt out - do not cut the threads. Fold the binding strip laying upward and lining up with the raw edge of the quilt. Hold the fold and lay the binding strip back down in line with the edge of the quilt (See diagrams) continue stitching. You should still be stitching on the raw edge of the binding and the quilt.

8 When you get back to near your starting point, stop, leaving a 3 - 5″ gap. Remove your project from your sewing machine. Open the binding strips and measure so that they meet at the middle point. Pin into place, again perpendicular (see Step 2) and sew. Trim with a ¼″ seam allowance. Finger press the seam open and continue to stitch in place.

9 Fold your binding over to the back side of your quilt, pin or clip into place, I use binding Clips, and hand stitch the binding down using a blind stitch and one strand of coordinating thread, mitre your corners as you go (refer to Hand and Embroidery Stitches in the techniques section.)

Projects

All My Love Doll Quilt

Every Doll deserves their own Quilt and what could be better
than one made with sweet hearts to show it was sewn with love.

FINISHED MEASUREMENTS
12" x 12"

Requirements

- One Hundred and Sixty-Nine 1" Jewel Papers and Template

- 1 Fat Quarter (18" x 21") White Background Fabric

- Five 6" squares of featured fabrics for the hearts or scraps for more variety

- Two 11" x 1" rectangles of floral border fabric

- Two 12" x 1" rectangles of floral border fabric

- 14" square of Backing Fabric

- 50" White Picot edge binding

- 14" square Quilt Batting or Pellon Fusible Fleece

- DMC Floss in White and 761 Pink

- Crochet Flower Trim (optional)

- "Created for You" Butterfly Charm (Optional)

- Basting Spray

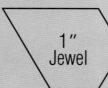

1"
Jewel

INSTRUCTIONS

1 Prepare 109 Jewels in the white background fabric and 60 Jewells in Coloured fabrics ready for English Paper Piecing. Refer to "English Paper Piecing" in the Techniques section. The Jewels made from the background fabrics can be 'strip cut' from the 21" side of the fat quarter. Refer to 'Cutting your EPP Shapes from Fabric' in the Techniques section.

2 English Paper piece two coloured Jewels together forming the coloured hearts. Repeat to create 30 heart units.

3 Begin to sew the white Jewels together forming rows to go in between the coloured heart rows as pictured.

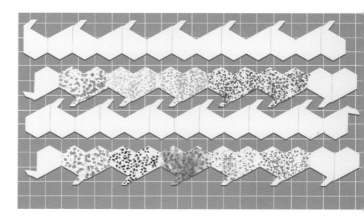

4 As you sew the Jewel shapes into rows, start to join the rows together to form the Doll Quilt. You need a total of thirteen rows. Once all your pieces and rows are sewn together remove all the papers, fold out the side seam allowance and gently press with an iron.

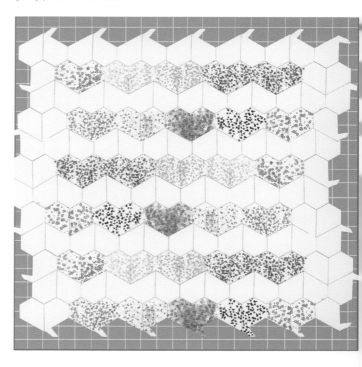

5 With a rotary cutter and patchwork ruler trim the panel back to 11" square.

6 With your sewing machine, sew around the outer edge of the mini quilt with a sort stitch and approx. ⅛" in from the edge. This will help secure any cut tread and stop your mini quilt from distortion.

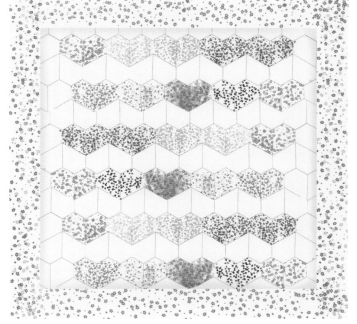

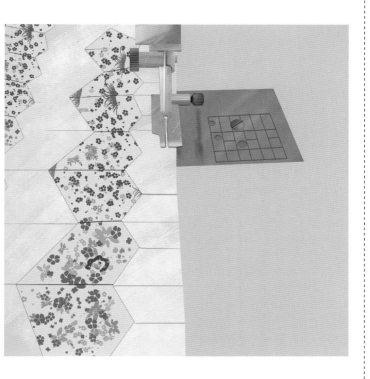

7 With a sewing machine, sew a 11" x 1" border rectangle to the top and the bottom of the mini quilt and then add a 12" x1" border strip to each side of the mini quilt. Press with an iron.

8 Baste the Mini quilt by laying the backing fabric, wrong side facing up, then the quilt batting (or Pellon) in the middle and the Mini Quilt top, on top, right side facing up. Spray baste as per the manufacturers instructions.

9 Hand quilt your Mini Doll Quilt. I have hand quilted ¼" inside the border in two strands of DMC 761, Pink and added three Lazy Daisies to each white row.

10 Bind the Mini Doll Quilt and add any other embellishments. I have added a White Crochet Flower and a small "Created for You" Charm. Refer to 'Binding' Patchwork and Quilting in the Techniques section.

A Stitch in Time Project Folder

Combining many of my loves, the cover of this project folder comes together like a 'Sampler' Quilt with a little mix of the different techniques explored within the pages of this book. When opened the folder reveals 4 zip pockets to store all your sewing supplies.

This is a fun project that will have you diving into your favourite scraps and finding that perfect vintage linen, lace or embellishment to make this project all your own, at the same time creating a beautiful project folder to take with you to your next sewing day or in your hand bag for sewing on the go.

FINISHED MEASUREMENTS
Closed Approximately 13" x 11.5"
Open Approximately 13" x 23"

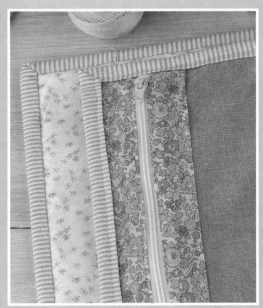

Requirements

- Twelve 2" Clamshell Papers and Template
- Five 1" Hexagon papers and Template
- Five 1" Half Hexagon papers and Template

THE COVER

- One 14" x 4" rectangle of white spot on white
- Twelve 2.5" squares of various fabrics for the Clamshells
- Ten 2.5" Squares various fabrics for the Hexagon Panel
- One 3" x 4.5" Rectangle (Vintage Linen)
- One 7" x 3" Soft Grey with White Spot
- One 4.5" square of Linen
- One 5.5" x 2" rectangle soft grey and white stripe
- Four 1.75" squares of various fabrics
- One 3.25" x 2" rectangle low volume print

- Crochet Doily for the top
- Two ¾" buttons
- 5.5" of a ¼" wide cream cotton lace trim
- 14" of a ¾" wide cream cotton lace trim
- 14" of a ¼" wide flower trim
- DMC Floss 739 Cream, 761 Candy Pink, 800 Blue
- One 3" x 12.5" rectangle of Pink Chambray for the Spine
- One 10.5" x 12.5" rectangle of White spot on Soft grey fabric for the back
- One 12.5" x 23" rectangle of Pellon Fusible Fleece
- Two 9.75" x 11.75" rectangles of Template Plastic
- One 1 7/8" x 11.75" rectangle Template Plastic
- 80" Binding

INSIDE THE FOLDER

- One 12.5" x 23" rectangle of a White Spot on Soft grey fabric
- Two 18" x 12.5" rectangles low volume fabric for larger pockets
- One 14" x 12.5" rectangles soft pink print fabrics for smaller pocket on left hand side
- One 14" x 9 ¼" rectangle in soft pink for the small pocket on the right-hand side
- 3.5" x 2.5" rectangle of pink felt
- Two 4.5" squares for scissor pocket or repurpose a vintage linen
- 8" of a ¾" wide cream cotton lace
- 13" Tape Measure Twill Tape
- Assortment of Vintage linens, lace and 2 small buttons to embellish small pocket.
- Small amount of Fibre Fill for Needle rest.

HANDMADE LABEL

- Two 3" squares low volume fabric
- 2" of a ¾" wide cream cotton lace
- 1 ½" Teddy Bear Leather Tag, handmade tag or Button

ZIP POCKETS

- One 11.5" x 20" Linen or suitable fabric that is 'double sided'
- Four 11.5" x 7.4" rectangles of Clear Vinyl
- Four 12" Zips
- Eight 1.5" x 2" rectangles for Zip Tabs
- Eight 13" x 1.5" rectangles for Zip sides
- Two 11.5" x 3" rectangles for centre pocket strips
- 68" of 2" Binding
- Millennium Pen
- Light Box
- Sewing Machine

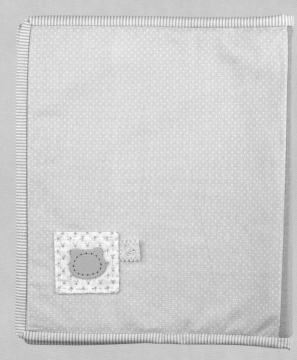

INSTRUCTIONS-THE COVER

CLAMSHELL PANEL

1 Prepare the 12 Clamshells ready for English Paper Piecing. Please refer to English Paper Piecing – Preparing shapes with curves in the Techniques section.

2 Fold the 14″ x 4″ rectangle in half along the 14″ length and gently press.

3 Centre and pin the 14″ length of cotton lace over the fold and with your sewing machine, sew into place by sewing along each side of the lace.

4 Centre and pin the 14″ length of flower trim to the centre of the lace and with your sewing machine, sew into place.

5 Join your clam shells into two rows of 6. Refer to "English Paper Piecing" and "Joining the Pieces – Clamshells", in the Techniques section.

6 Applique one set of the clamshells to each side of the 14″ length aligning the base of the main clamshell curve with the edge of the background fabric. (This length of fabric will be trimmed back to 12.5″ in the next step.) The top of the Clamshells should sit approx. ¼″ from the edge of the cotton lace but this could vary dependant on the actual width of lace you have used. Ensure that the clamshells on each side line up with each other. Once done, carefully remove the papers and gently iron the panel.

7 Trim the clamshell panel to 12.5″ x 4″ and set aside.

HEXAGON PANEL

8 Prepare the 5 Hexagons and 5 Half Hexagons ready for English Paper Piecing and proceed to sew them together (Use photos as a guide). Refer to "English Paper Piecing" in the Techniques section.

9 Remove all the papers, fold the seam allowances open and gently press with a warm iron and with a rotary cutter and ruler trim the hexagon panel back to 7″ x 3 ¼″.

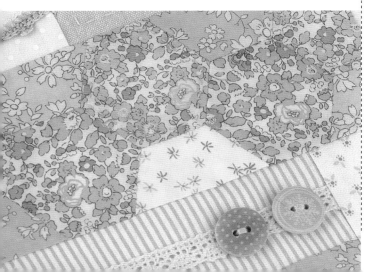

PATCHWORK

10 If you are using a Vintage linen with a crochet edge, first lay the linen over a low volume square of fabric and sew into place. Trim away the excess low volume fabric from the back and then trim the rectangle to 3″ x 4.5″.

11 Using the layout diagram as a guide, with your sewing machine sew the following. Please note: This diagram is not to scale and shows the 'cut' measurements.

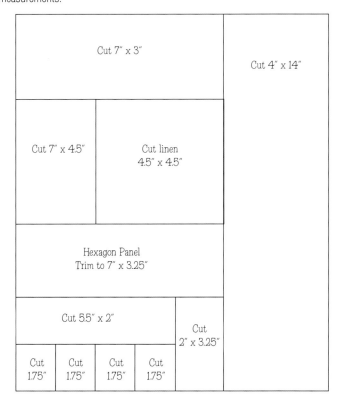

Cut 7″ x 3″	Cut 4″ x 14″
Cut 7″ x 4.5″ / Cut linen 4.5″ x 4.5″	
Hexagon Panel Trim to 7″ x 3.25″	
Cut 5.5″ x 2″	Cut 2″ x 3.25″
Cut 1.75″ / Cut 1.75″ / Cut 1.75″ / Cut 1.75″	

A- Sew the 3″ x 4.5″ vintage linen rectangle to the 4.5″ square of linen, press the

45

seams and then sew the 7" x 3" rectangle of white spot on soft grey to the top and the 7" x 3 ¼" hexagon panel to the bottom. Press the seams.

B- Centre a 5.5" length of ¼" wide cotton lace along the length of the soft grey stripe 5.5" x 2" rectangle and sew into place with a sewing machine.

C- Sew the four 1.75" squares together and then sew the 5.5" x 2" lace embellished rectangle to the top of the squares. Press the seams and then sew the 3 ¼" x 2" low volume rectangle to the right-hand side of the unit. Press the seams.

D- Sew the Clamshell unit (finished at Step 7) to the right-hand side and press the panel.

12 Pin your chosen Doily into place at the top of the pieced panel and with your sewing machine, sew just inside the edge to secure into place BEFORE trimming away any excess sew across the top with a ⅛" seam to secure.

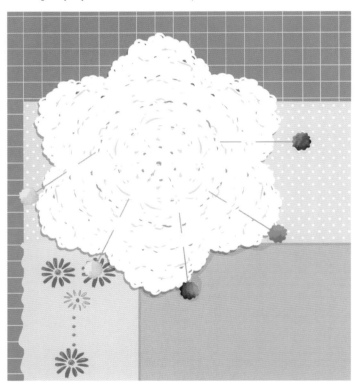

13 Using a light box and a Millennium Pen, trace the Embroidery from the template page onto the blank Linen square.

14 Using a Back Stitch and a Long and Short Stitch as a filler, embroider the design using a DMC Floss #900. Add hand quilting details in DMC Floss #761 Candy Pink and #739 Cream. Sew in the two buttons and any other embellishments that you may like to add.

15 With a sewing machine, sew the 3" x 12.5" Pink Chambray rectangle to the right-hand side of the Patchwork panel.

16 Sew the 10.5" x 12.5" rectangle of white spot on soft grey fabric to the left of the pink chambray. Your complete front and back cover of the folder should now measure 12.5" x 23"

17 Following the manufactures instructions, iron the 12.5" x 23" piece of Pellon to the back of the folder.

HANDMADE LABEL

18 Face the two 3" squares right side facing and sew all the way around the edge.

19 With a pair of scissors, carefully cut a 'X' in the back of one square. Turn the square right sides out through the 'X' and Press.

20 Centre the Leather tag (or handmade tag / button etc.) to the centre of the square and sew into place.

21 Position the handmade tag at your preferred position, on what will be the back of the folder. Fold the 2" length of lace in half and pin into place ensuring that the ends will be caught when the tag is sewn in into place.

22 Sew the handmade label into place by hand or with a sewing machine.

23 Set the cover aside.

INSIDE FOLDER UNIT

24 Take the two 18" x 12.5" rectangles and fold in half making two 9" x 12.5" rectangles and press. With a sewing machine topstitch ¼" in from the fold on both. These are now the two large pockets.

25 Lay the 12.5" x 23" rectangle of white spot on soft grey fabric right side facing up and lay one of the large pockets made above on each side with the folded/topstitched edge facing in.

26 Take the 14" x 12.5" rectangle of soft pink fabric and fold it in half making a 7" x 12.5" rectangle. Press and with a sewing machine topstitch ¼" in from the folded seam. This is the small, narrower pocket for the left-hand side of the folder.

27 Create a 4" square pocket from vintage linens, a repurposed coaster or two 4.5" squares.

A- Refer to Step 11 if creating a panel from a crochet edge linen. Alternatively cut a 4.5" square from a vintage linen and a 4.5" square from a second fabric for the pocket lining.

B- Face the two 4.5" squares right sides together and sew around all the sides leaving a 2" turning gap in the bottom. Snip away excess fabric at the corners and turn the pocket right sides out and press.

C- Using a whip stitch, sew the turning gap closed.

28 Position and pin the scissor pocket into place by centring it 2" up from the bottom.

29 Cut a 2" length from the 8" length of ¾" wide cotton lace and pin it under the pocket on the right-hand side. With a sewing machine, sew down the two sides and along the bottom of the pocket leaving the top open.

30 Use the remaining 6" length of cotton lace trim to embellish the bottom of the pocket, folding under the ends of the lace and sewing into place with a sewing machine.

31 (Optional) If you would like to add any other embellishments such as the scissors pictured, sew them into place now.

32 Copy the Needle rest shape from the template page onto paper and pin it to the pink felt and using scissors, cut out the shape.

33 Pin the felt needle rest shape to the top half of the small pocket and using a running stitch, sew into place. Add a small amount of Fibre Fill before finishing to give the needle rest a little height. Careful not to overstuff. See 'Hand and Embroidery Stitches' in the Techniques section.

34 Lay the 'needle rest' pocket on top of the large pocket to the left-hand side of the inside folder unit. Pin the layers into place. (See picture at Step 40)

35 Take the 14" x 9 ¼" rectangle of soft pink fabric and fold it in half, right sides facing, making a 9 ¼" x 7" rectangle. With the fold at the top sew a seam along the left-hand side. Clip the corner. Turn right sides out and Press.

36 Topstitch ¼" down from the folded seam. This is the small pocket for the right-hand side of the folder.

37 Embellish the pocket any way you like. I have used a vintage crochet doily which had a small hole in the centre. I covered the centre with a partial embroidered doily, lace trim and two small buttons.

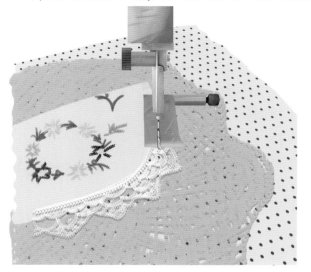

38 Lay the completed small pocket on top of the large pocket made for the right-hand side. Pin and sew the length of tape measure twill tape to the left-hand side of the pockets pinning all the layers together. (See picture at Step 40).

39 Pin the completed unit to the right-hand side of the inside folder unit and pin in place.

40 With your sewing machine, sew around the entire outside of the inside folder/pocket unit with a ⅛" seam to secure all the pockets etc.

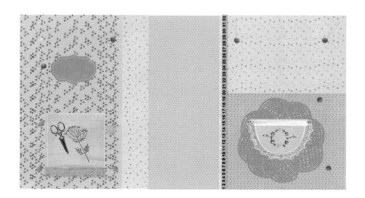

ZIP POCKETS

The pockets for this unit are going to be sewn to each side of the Linen 11.5" x 20" rectangle. I have chosen a Linen as it can be used as a double-sided fabric, i.e. no wrong or right side. If you are not using Linen or a double-sided fabric you may choose to fuse two layers of fabric together. When creating this unit, you may find it helpful to pin the pockets in place to each side of the linen so that you can see where they go and to ensure that you are sewing the pockets in the correct direction with the zip openings at the top and with the zip to the outer edge of the linen.

41 Trim away the metal end on all four zips and oversew the ends closed with your sewing machine. This is an optional step but one I always like to do as removing the metal decreases the potential risk of damage to your sewing machine if you did accidently happen to hit it whilst sewing.

42 Sew a 1.5" x 2" rectangle to the end of your zip by taking a tab, fold under one of the 1.5" ends by ¼" and sew it to the end of the zip.

43 Open the zip and then measure 10.5" from the tab and trim off the excess.

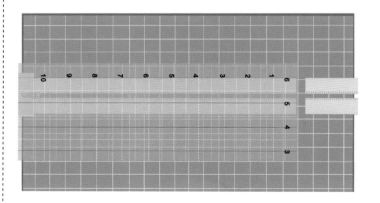

44 Sew the zip end closed with your sewing machine and repeat Step 42 for this end of the zip.

45 With a Zipper foot on your sewing machine, sew a 13″ x 1.5″ rectangle to each side of the zip. Fold back the fabric and topstitch. Repeat for all four zips.

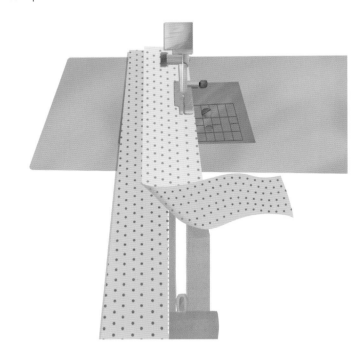

46 Trim the four zip units back to 11.5″ in length.

TIPS FOR WORKING WITH THE CLEAR VINYL

When sewing with clear vinyl, it can 'stick' to the work surface on your sewing machine. To help avoid this:

- Ensure your feed dogs are clean so that they can grip the vinyl as you sew.

- Sew with the vinyl facing down on the feed dogs, NOT up under the foot of your sewing machine.

- With your left hand hold the vinyl up so that it does not rest on the work surface of your sewing machine.

- Go slow and allow your sewing machine to feed through the vinyl.

- If it is still sticking, layer a piece of paper, as if it was an extra layer of fabric, holding it in place with binding clips so that it sits between your sewing machine and the vinyl. Sew with a shorter stitch and when finished, carefully tear away the paper. Baking paper or foundation paper works great.

47 Lay the completed zip units on your workspace. Ensure that the zips are closed and the zipper pull is at the top. Sew a clear vinyl rectangle to each Unit ensuring that TWO zip units have the vinyl sewn to the right and TWO have the vinyl sewn to the Left.

48 Trim the zip and vinyl units so they measure 11.5″ x 9″.

49 To create the larger zip/vinyl units for each side of the linen you need to sew a 11.5″ x 3″ rectangle between two of the zip/vinyl units. Lay the fabric right sides facing the vinyl and sew. Open and then topstitch. Sew another zip/vinyl unit to the right-hand side of the 11.5″ x 3″ rectangle. Open and topstitch. Repeat for the second of the larger zip/vinyl units for the reverse side of the linen.

50 Pin the two pocket units to each side of the Linen. Only pin through the fabric NOT the clear vinyl. Ensure that the zip openings are at the top.

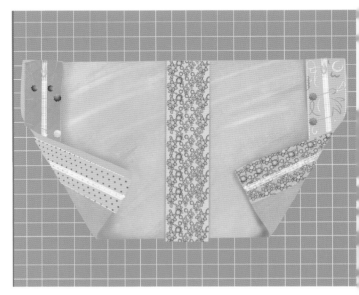

51 Using a ⅛″ seam sew around this unit on the FABRIC ONLY, sewing together the three layers.

52 Machine bind around the complete zip pocket unit. We are machine binding this unit because of the clear vinyl. Using Binding Clips, pin the binding around the outside of the pocket unit, mitring the corners as you go taking care to line up both sides of the binding evenly to ensure that both sides of the binding are caught when you sew.

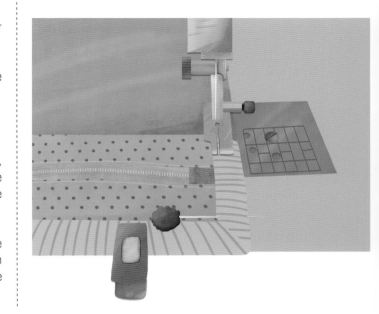

THE FINAL ASSEMBLY

53 With a water erasable pen mark the centre of the double-sided zip pocket panel. Line this up with the centre of the inside folder unit. Pin into place. With a sewing machine sew ¼″ each side of the centre line. Remove the centre marking.

54 Pin the cover and inside folder units together with right sides facing out with your sewing machine, sew ¼″ inside the centre spine of the cover, ensuring that the centre zip pockets are out of the way.

55 With a ⅛″ seam, sew along both sides and the top of the folder, leaving the bottom open.

56 Slide the template plastic in between the two layers of the cover. Ensuring that they are pushed towards the top, sew along the bottom of the folder, again with a ⅛″ seam.

57 Bind your folder, starting at the back where the join will be less obvious. When sewing your binding ensure that you are sliding the template plastic away from the seam you are sewing as you do not want to sew through the template plastic. Finish your binding by hand. Refer to "Binding" in the Techniques section.

Enjoy your new "A Stitch in Time Project Folder".

Dahlia Candle Mat

A sweet little Candle mat which could also be used
under a vase, cake plate or on your dressing table.
The choice is yours. Have fun and explore the
fussy cutting opportunities that this design allows.

FINISHED MEASUREMENTS
Approximately 11" diameter

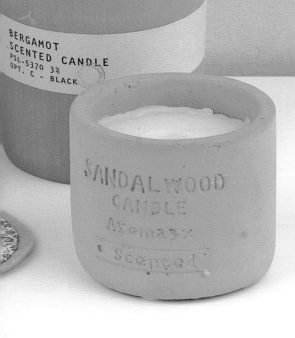

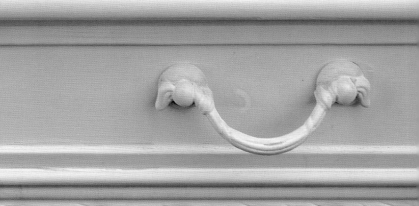

Requirements

- Twenty-Four 1" 8 point Diamond Papers
- Eight 1" Square Papers
- Sixteen 1" Half Square Triangle Papers
- Eight Dahlia Half Square Triangle Papers*
- Sixteen Dahlia Petal Papers*

*Please note that the Dahlia Half Square Triangles and Petals are a custom shape. Please read the note on "Custom Shapes" in the English Paper Piecing Techniques Section.

- 12" square of Wool Felt
- Fat Quarter of a central fabric. (If fussy cutting you may require more fabric, please ensure you have a minimum repeat of 8.)
- 10" Square of a Low Volume Fabric
- 10" Mauve Solid Fabric
- 10" Square of Hot Pink Printed Fabric
- 12" Square of Floral printed fabric for Petals.

INSTRUCTIONS

1 Prepare your Dahlia papers by tracing or copying the shapes from the template pages onto 160gsm card and cut out your papers ready for English Paper Piecing. Please refer to "English Paper Piecing" in the Techniques Section.

2 Prepare all your shapes so they are ready for English Paper Piecing. Please note that of your 16 Dahlia Petal papers you need to prepare/baste eight Dahlia Petals as pictured on the template page and another eight in REVERSE to complete the outer petal design. The centre of your Dahlia Candle Mat allows you to play with some kaleidoscope fussy cutting. Please refer to "English Paper Piecing" and "Fussy Cutting" in the Techniques section for some ideas and techniques on how to achieve some amazing effects with your fabrics. If you wish to make your own templates for the custom shapes please refer to "Creating a Template" in the Techniques section.

3 Begin to piece your Candle Mat in sections, starting with your centre 8 point diamonds. It is important to join the centre in two sections of four and then join these two sections together forming the centre unit. This helps to ensure that your centre points all meet neatly, thus giving you a neater finish.

4 Breaking a project down into smaller sections, as pictured, will make piecing your Candle mat easier to handle. Once you have completed the entire 8 point diamond star, work your way around adding the 1" squares and then work your way around again adding the 1" 8 pointed diamonds.

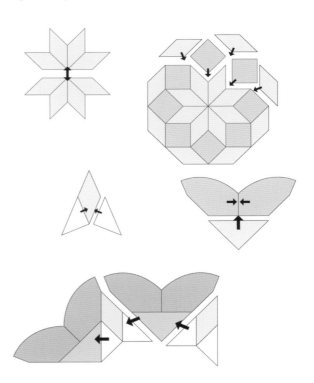

Sew a 1" half square triangle to each side of an 8 point diamond, make 8 units.

Piece your Dahlia Half Square triangle and Dahlia Petal units as pictured, make 8 units.

Piece 4 units from these Dahlia petal units and diamond units as pictured. At this stage, your Candle Mat has a total of 5 easy to manage units that can now be sewn together.

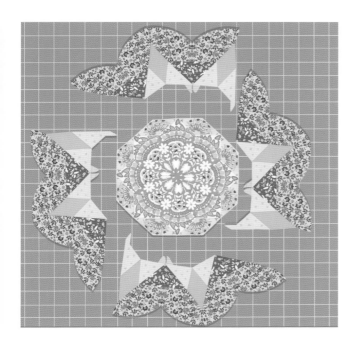

6 Enlarge the Felt Background Template by 200% and use it to cut out your felt background ready to applique your panel to.

7 Lay your EPP Panel right sides down on your work surface and apply small dots of Applique glue to the seam allowance around the outer edge of your work.

8 Carefully flip back over and centre your EPP Panel onto the felt background and allow the applique glue to dry.

9 Applique your EPP Panel to your felt background using a Blind Stitch. Refer to "Hand and Embroidery Stitches" in the Techniques Section. Your Candle Mat is now ready to use.

5 Once you have pieced your candle mat into one piece gently press with an iron and remove all the papers. Press again if required.

Dumpling Bag

A beautiful drawstring bag on a pentagon base.
Ready to keep your sewing or newest crochet
project safe and together.

FINISHED MEASUREMENTS
Approximately 9 ¼" x 11"

Requirements

- Ninety ¾″ Hexagon Papers
- Fifteen 2″ Clamshell Papers
- Various fabrics for the Hexagons and Clamshells
- Five 6.5″ x 9″ rectangles of Feature Floral Fabric for behind the pockets
- One Pentagon Base in Feature Floral Fabric
- Five 6.5″ x 2.5″ rectangles in Cream fabric
- Five 6.5″ x 1.25″ rectangles in Cream fabric
- Five 5 ¾″ x 6.5″ rectangles in a Pink contrast fabric for pocket lining
- Five 6.5″ x 9″ rectangle in Pink Gingham for the pleats
- One 8″ x 30.5″ rectangle in Pink Gingham for bag top
- Two 2.5″ x 15″ rectangles in a Pink Floral for casings
- One 9″ x 30.5″ rectangle in a Solid Pink fabric for the lining
- One Pentagon Base in Solid Pink Fabric for the lining
- One Pentagon Base from Template plastic
- Two Pentagon Bases from scrap batting
- 86″ Double Sided Satin Ribbon
- 'Handmade' Leather Tag

INSTRUCTIONS

1 Copy the Dumpling Bag 'Base' Template from the Templates section onto copy paper or card and use it to cut the exterior bag base, lining base, template plastic base and wadding.

2 Prepare the hexagons and clamshells for English Paper Piecing. Please refer to "English Paper Piecing" in the Techniques section.

CREATING THE POCKETS

3 Play with the layout of your hexagons so that you have five groups of eighteen hexagons and sew each group together in six columns of three.

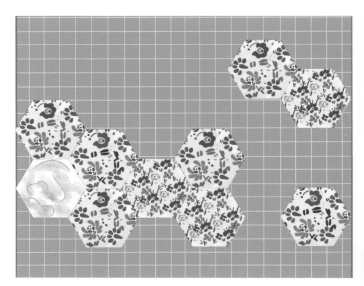

4 For each of the five panels remove the papers, fold out the seam allowances on outer hexagons and gently press your panels with an iron.

5 Trim your Hexagon Panels to 6.5″ wide and 3.5″ high. You will NOT need to cut through any of your hand stitching. Set aside.

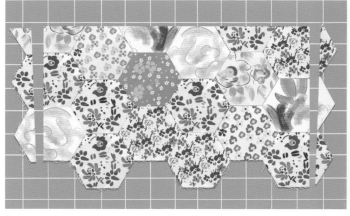

6 Sew your Clamshells together in groups of three as per the "Joining the Pieces – Clamshells" in the Techniques Section.

7 With your sewing machine, sew a 6.5″ x 2.5″ cream fabric to the bottom of a 5 ¾″ x 6.5″ Contrast Pink Pocket lining fabric and press. Repeat for all five. Set aside.

8 Following the instructions in the "English Paper Piecing Techniques section – Joining the pieces – Clamshells", applique your clamshells to the cream fabric referenced in step 7 with the top of the clamshells sitting just under the pocket fabric.

9 Remove the papers and using a rotary cutter and patchwork ruler, trim off the bottom of the clamshells by measuring down 1 ¼" from the seam of the cream and pocket lining fabric.

10 With your sewing machine, sew the 6.5" x 1.25" cream fabric to the bottom of the clamshells with right sides together. Repeat for all five.

11 Sew one of the English Paper Pieced Hexagon panels to the bottom of the cream strip. Repeat for all five pockets.

12 Iron your pocket panels in half, right sides facing out so that you have the pocket lining fabric forming a trim at the top of the pocket.

13 Pin and then sew the pocket to the bottom of the 6.5" x 9" feature fabric using a scant ¼" seam so it won't be seen later when assembling the bag. Repeat for all five pockets.

CREATING THE DUMPLING BAG EXTERIOR

14 Alternating from a pleat panel to a pocket panel sew the ten pieces together forming one long panel. As you go fold the pleat fabric under the pocket and topstitch with a ¼" seam.

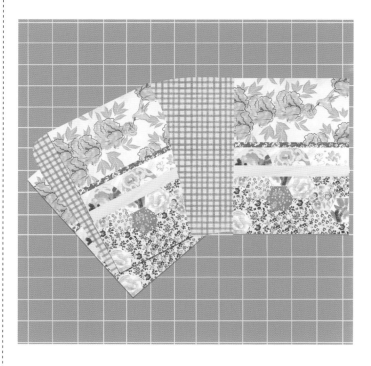

15 Create the pleat in the check print fabric by bringing together two pockets. Pin into place and with your sewing machine stitch along the top and bottom of the pleats with a scant ¼" seam to secure the pleats.

16 With your iron, press the pleats from the back.

17 With your sewing machine, sew the two ends of the bag together and finish off the last pleat.

The exterior of your Dumpling Bag should now be a cylinder.

18 With a water erasable pen, copy the dots from the template sheet to the wrong side of the bag base. Line up the bottom of one pocket with one side of the pentagon and pin into place. Place the panel/base in your sewing machine with the base facing up so that you can see your dots. Start sewing at one dot and sew to the next dot, backstitch at the end and remove from your machine. Pin the next side by again lining the bottom of the pocket with the edge of the base, pinning and sewing between the dots. Repeat for all sides.

CREATING THE CASING PANEL

19 Take the 8" x 30.5" pink gingham strip and sew the two 8" sides together to form a loop.

20 Press in half, right sides facing out so that your loop is now 4" in height.

21 Take the two 2.5" x 15" strips and fold each short end over ¼" and press. Fold over another ¼" and press then top stitch.

22 Fold each strip in half lengthways, right sides of fabric facing and with a sewing machine sew the long side of each unit forming two long cylinders. Turn right sides out and press with the seam to the back. These will be the casings for the drawstring ribbon.

23 Fold the pink gingham in half, centre one casing 1 ¼" up from the bottom and pin into place ensuring that you only pin to one side (two layers of fabric). Repeat for the other side of the gingham strip.

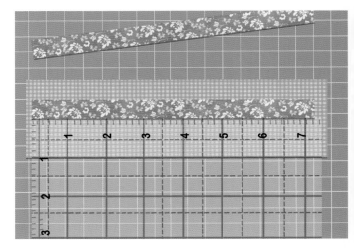

24 Topstitch the long sides of the two casing strips into place close to the edge of the casing strips. (Leave the short ends open).

25 Find the quarter way points around the bag and the Casing Panel completed above. Pin the casing panel into place around the top of the bag ensuring that the casing panel is on the outside of the bag and both units have their right sides facing each other.

26 Sew the casing panel into place with a scant ¼" seam.

27 Measure up 1" from the base of your bag at each pleat / pocket, join and hand stitch two little cross stitches, using two strands of a coordinating DMC Thread, catching two pockets.

28 Optional - If you wish to add a Handmade tag to your bag you might like to add it now or alternatively add it when your bag is finished.

CREATING THE LINING

29 Take the 9" x 30.5" Light Solid Pink fabric for the lining and sew the two 9" sides together.

30 With pins or a water erasable marker, mark 6" intervals on the bottom of the lining cylinder starting at the seam and working your way around. Follow step 18 to sew the lining base to the lining cylinder, leaving one side open for the turning gap. The 6" interval markings represent the pockets/sides of the bag for lining up the pentagon base.

31 With your bag exterior right side facing out and your casing panel folded down to the outside of the bag, and your lining wrong side facing out, slide your bag exterior into the lining so that the right sides of both the bag and lining are facing ensuring that you match the corners of the lining and outer bag. Align the bag top and the lining, remembering that the casing panel is folded down, and pin into place. With your sewing machine, sew with a quarter inch seam all the way around.

32 Turn your bag right sides out through the turning gap.

33 Working your way around the bag, and ensuring that the lining lays flat on the inside, pin the lining to the bag and then topstitch with your sewing machine.

TEMPLATE BASE

34 Sandwich the Template Plastic Base between the two Pentagon bases cut from scrap batting and pin. With your sewing machine, carefully sew around the template base ensuring that you do not sew through the template plastic.

35 Turn your bag back to wrong sides facing out and using a whip stitch or running stitch sew your Template plastic base into place by sewing the batting to the seam allowance to secure into place. Binding clips can help hold the base in place as you sew. Refer to "Hand and Embroidery Stitches" in the Techniques Section.

36 Turn your bag right side out again and slip stitch the lining closed.

37 Cut the Satin ribbon in half creating two 43" lengths.

38 Place a safety pin in one end of the ribbon and use it to thread the ribbon from one side of the bag, through both casings back to the start. Remove the Safety pin and knot the end. Take other ribbon and repeat the process but this time start from the opposite side, thread through both casings, back to the start and knot. Your Dumpling Bag is now ready to use.

Guest Set
Bath and Hand Towels

Having guests come to stay is always special, so why not make them a special Guest Set that they can take home with them to remember their time spent with you in your home. This set would also be nice for someone going off to college, moving out of home for the first time, a new baby or an engagement present.

Requirements

BATH TOWEL

- Fourteen 1" Hexagon papers
- One Standard Sized Bath Towel
- One 10" square of a Cream Print Fabric
- One 10" square of a Green Print Fabric
- Two 2.5" squares of Pink solid fabric
- 28" Cotton Lace Trim that is wide enough to cover the band on the towel. *
- 12" x 6" piece of Double sided fusible web / Visofix

HAND TOWEL

- Fourteen ½" Hexagon Papers
- One Standard Sized Hand Towel
- One 6" square of a Cream Print Fabric
- One 6" square of a Green Print Fabric
- Two 1.5" squares of Pink solid fabric
- 14" Cotton Lace Trim that is wide enough to cover the band on the towel. *
- 2.5" x 5" piece of double sided fusible web / Visofix

*Due to Towel size variations please check the overall width of your towels to ensure you have purchased / have enough of the Cotton Lace Trim.

The instructions for both the Bath and Hand Towel are the same it is just the size of the hexagons and length of the cotton lace trim that differs.

INSTRUCTIONS

1 Prepare your Hexagons ready for English Paper Piecing – Please refer to "English Paper Piecing" in the Techniques Section.

2 English paper piece your hexagons together to form your flower. There is no wrong or right order in which to sew a hexagon flower together and here is one suggestion. Please refer to "English Paper Piecing" in the techniques section for full instructions.

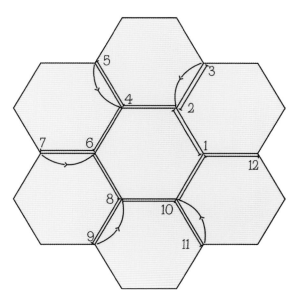

3 With your iron, gently press your hexagon flowers and then remove the papers.

4 Trace two of the corresponding full hexagon flower shapes found on the template page for this project onto the paper side of your Visofix / Double sided fusible web and cut out with your scissors. These shapes are slightly smaller than your finished hexagon flower.

5 Iron on the Visofix to the centre of the wrong side of your hexagon flower following the manufacturer's instructions ensuring that your seam allowance has been pressed flat. Set aside.

6 Measure the width of your towel / hand towel and cut a piece of Cotton Lace 1" longer.

7 With your sewing machine, sew the cotton lace to the towel over the towel band. Start at one end by folding the cotton lace under ½" and pin into place. Continue to pin across the width of the towel folding the other short end under ½". With your sewing machine, sew the cotton lace into position all the way around.

8 Take your towel and flowers to your ironing board. Remove the paper from the fusible web on the back of the two hexagon flowers. Position the flowers, right side up anywhere you like along the towel width, overlapping the lace. When you are happy with your positioning use your iron to press into place.

9 With your sewing machine and coordinating thread, top stitch the flowers into place approx. ⅛" inside the edge of the hexagons.

Your towel is now ready to be gifted.

Little Miss Sweetness Bag

This sweet little bag is sure to inspire many hours of imaginary play for that special little person in your life.

FINISHED MEASUREMENTS
Approximately 8" x 10.5"

Requirements

- Thirty-One ¾" Octagon Papers and Template
- Twenty-eight ¾" Square papers
- Fabric for Fussy Cutting the Octagons and Squares
- 12" x 10" Pink Gingham for Bag back exterior
- 3" x 26" Pink Gingham for Bag gusset
- Two 3.5" x 38" Pink Gingham for bag handles
- Two 12" x 10" Pink fabric for bag lining
- 2.5" x 24.5" Pink Fabric for gusset lining
- Soft and Stable
    - Two 12" x 10" rectangles
    - One 3" x 26" rectangle
- Leather 'Handmade' Tag (optional)
- Basting Spray
- Sewing machine with a Walking Foot

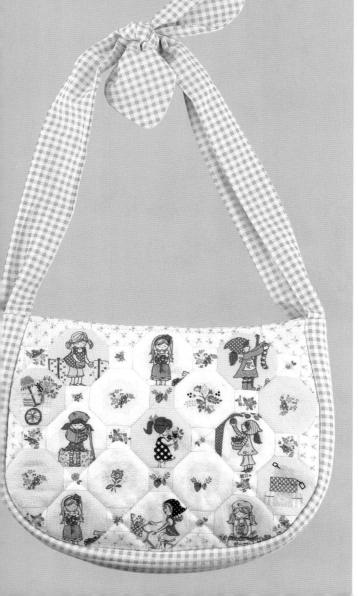

INSTRUCTIONS

1 Photocopy or trace the Bag body and the Bag handle template from the template pages onto card or copy paper and cut out along the line ready for use.

TIP: Copy the Bag template twice and tape together to make one large full sized template. This will make the cutting out your bag shapes from the quilted panels easier.

2 Prepare the 31 Octagons and 28 squares ready for English Paper Piecing. The squares and octagons on the outside of the English Paper Pieced panel will be cut into when trimming the panel to create the bag front so please take this into consideration if you plan to fussy cut all your pieces.

3 Play with the layout of your Octagons and squares. Once you are happy, English Paper Piece your panel together. Refer to "English Paper Piecing" in the Techniques Section.

4 Once completed, remove all the papers, fold out the seam allowances around the outer edge of the panel and gently press with a warm iron.

5 Following the manufacturer's instructions, spray baste the English Paper Pieced panel to one of the 12" x 10" rectangles of Soft and Stable.

6 Repeat for the 12" x 10" Pink Gingham bag exterior and spray baste it to the remaining 12" x 10" piece of Soft and Stable.

7 Spray baste the 3" x 26" Pink Gingham for the Bag exterior gusset to the 3" x 26" piece of Soft and Stable.

8 With your sewing machine and a Walking Foot, quilt the two bag exterior panels. I have used a diagonal grid based on the diagonal lines of the octagons. For the long gusset piece, straight line quilt the entire length with a spacing of approximately ¼" to ½"

9 Using the "Bag Template" prepared at Step 1, cut one bag shape from both the English Paper Pieced Panel and the Quilted bag back panel. Set aside.

10 With a Rotary cutter and ruler trim the quilted bag gusset back to 2.5″ x 24.5″.

11 Placing the bag front, right sides facing with the bag gusset, pin into place all the way around from one side to the other.

12 With a Sewing machine, sew the two pieces together with a ¼″ seam allowance.

13 Repeat by pinning the bag back, right sides facing the other side of the bag gusset and sew into place.

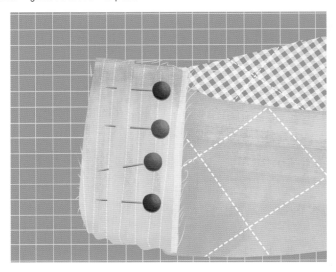

14 Optional – If you are adding a "Handmade" tag to the back of your bag, hand stitch it into place now.

15 Using the Bag template cut two of the bag panels from the lining fabric.

16 Repeat steps 11 and 12 to start make the bag lining, this time using a regular foot on your sewing machine.

17 When sewing the second bag panel to the gusset leave a 4″ turning gap at the bottom, back stitching at each start stop point.

CREATING THE HANDLES

18 Take the two 3.5″ x 38″ pink gingham bag handle pieces and fold each in half, right sides facing, creating two 3.5″ x 19″ rectangles.

19 At the fold ends lay the Bag handle template made at Step 1 on the fabric and trace the curve of the template with a water erasable pen or a pencil.

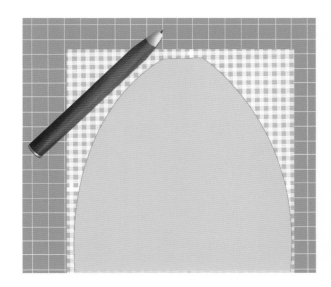

20 Trim away the excess fabric along the drawn line.

21 With your sewing machine, sew along both long lengths on each side of the two handles and around the curve ensuring that the short straight end is left open.

22 With your scissors, snip into the seam allowance around the curve ensuring that you do not snip into the sewn seam.

23 Turn the handles right side out and press with an iron.

ASSEMBLING THE BAG

24 Take the outer shell of the bag and pin one handle to each side in-between the gusset/bag seams, pleating the bag handle to fit.

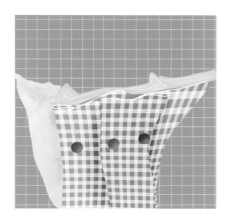

25 With your sewing machine and using a ⅛″ seam allowance, sew the handles into place.

26 Have the exterior of the bag right sides facing out and slide the lining up over the bag exterior so that both the bag exterior and lining are right sides facing. Ensure that the handles are tucked down and out of the way, pin the two bag pieces together lining up the seams and with your sewing machine sew around the top of the bag.

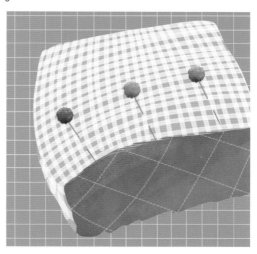

27 Turn the bag right sides out through the turning gap left in the lining at Step 17.

28 Work your way around the top of the bag pinning the exterior and lining down so that the top seam is neat and with a sewing machine, top stitch around the top of the bag.

29 Turn the bag so the interior is facing out. With some coordinating thread Slip Stitch the turning gap closed and then sew the lining gusset to the Soft and Stable in the seam allowance of the bag exterior to hold the lining in place. Refer to "Hand and Embroidery Stitches" in the Techniques section for the stitch guide.

30 Tie the handles together towards the ends and you have finished.

Miss Dolly

Miss Dolly would be the perfect new friend for that special little person in your life.

FINISHED MEASUREMENTS
11" Tall

Requirements

- Seven ¼" Hexagon Papers
- One 8" x 11" rectangle of Pink Wool Felt
- One 8" x 14" rectangle of Skin Toned Wool Felt
- Two 6" x 7" rectangle of Light Blue Wool Felt
- 3" Square of floral fabric for flower
- DMC Floss BLANC – White, 225 Soft Pink
- 5" White Picot Edge Binding
- 20" of ½" wide Cotton Lace
- Fibre Fill / Toy Stuffing
- Turning Tool (eg, 'Purple Thang')
- Light Box

INSTRUCTIONS

1 Trace or copy the Doll Pieces from the templates pages. Cut the required number of pieces from the felt as per the instructions on the pattern pieces ensuring that you cut along the solid cut lines. The perforated lines indicate the ¼" seam allowance and guides for lining the hair to the face and the head to the dress pieces.

2 With a sewing machine, sew the two dress back pieces together leaving open a turning gap in the centre of the seam. Backstitch at the start and end of each seam.

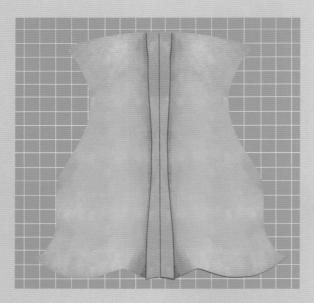

3 Overlap the face and hair as indicated on the pattern pieces and pin into place. Repeat for the hair and head back pieces. With a sewing machine, sew the pieces together on the overlap in a coordinating thread.

4 Use the guide marks on the pattern pieces to align the head and dress pieces together. Pin into place. With a sewing machine, sew the headpieces to the body pieces. The one-piece dress unit is sewn to the head front and the two-pieced dress unit is sewn to the head back.

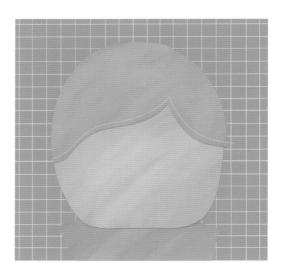

5 Layer and pin the three layers of the pigtail units together. With a sewing machine sew just inside the edge of the pigtails and then another two lines inside that for texture.

6 Pin the pigtails into place on the head front and then with a ⅛" seam allowance, sew into place.

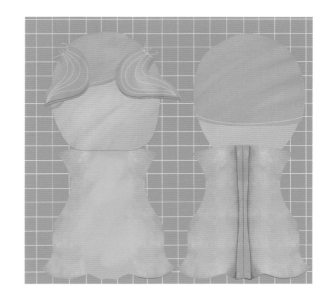

7 Pin the arm and leg units together and with a quarter inch seam allowance sew around the outside leaving the seam at the top of the arms and legs open. Carefully with pointy ended scissors, clip around the curves of the arm and leg units. Using a turning tool, turn the arms and legs right sides out and then stuff with fibrefill approximately ¾ of the way.

8 Prepare and sew the ¼" hexagons into a flower. Remove the papers and press with a warm iron. Refer to 'English Paper Piecing' in the Techniques section.

9 Using the hexagon flower on the dress template as a guide, applique the hexagon flower into place.

10 Using DMC Floss in BLANC (White) embroider two lazy daisy stitches and a French knot in each position around the flower. Please refer to 'Embroidery Stitches' in the Techniques section.

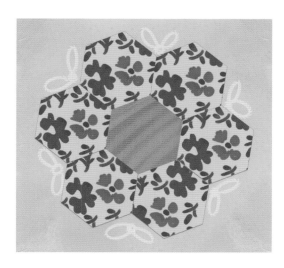

11 Using a light box, trace the face onto the doll. You can embroider eyes, circles or half circles, or cut circles from the felt and stitch into place with a running stitch depending on your personal preference for your dolls expression.

For a fuller lip, embroider a 'split stitch' or for a softer lip use a 'running stitch'.

12 Pin the arm and legs into position. The arms need to be positioned just over ¼" down from the shoulder of the dress. Ensure that the thumbs are positioned facing up. The legs need to be centred over the curve indent points on the bottom of the dress. Sew the arms and legs into place using a ⅛" seam allowance.

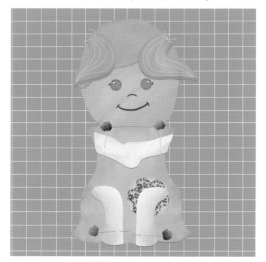

13 Fold the tips at the end of the pigtails towards the centre of the head and pin into place with the pin being at the back (wrong side) of the head. (We are pinning the pigtails out of the way so that they do not get caught in the seams when sewing the two doll pieces together.)

14 Facing the doll front and doll back, right sides together, line up the edges and pin into place. Slowly and carefully with a sewing machine, sew around the entire circumference of the doll, removing the pins as you go. Before turning your doll right sides out double check the seam to make sure that you have caught both layers of felt. If you have missed a spot, go back over it with the sewing machine.

15 Remove the pins that are holding the pigtails in pace. Slowly turn your doll right sides out through the turning gab at the back of the dress and gently feeding one pigtail and then the other through the neck seam.

16 Firmly fill the doll with fibre fill and using a slip stitch, sew the turning gap at the back of the dress closed. Refer 'Hand and Embroidery Stitches' in the Techniques section.

DRESSING THE DOLL

17 Take the length of Picot Edge Binding and using a whip stitch sew it around the neck of the doll forming a collar for the dress. Overlap the edges, trim to length and secure into place.

18 Centre the cotton lace trim around the waist of the doll and again using a slip stitch secure into place. Finish off by tying into a bow at the back and trim to length. She is now ready to play.

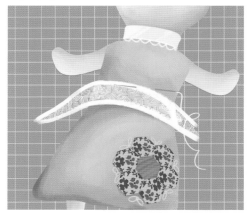

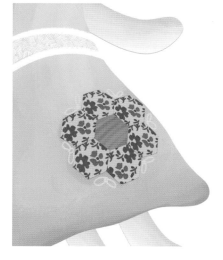

Mummy Rosie and Miss Lucy
the Mouse Pincushion

Everyone needs cute little friends to keep them company and both Mummy Rosie and Miss Lucy are here to keep you, or a friend company as you stitch the day away. They may be a little too cute to use and I see them both needing a friend or two.

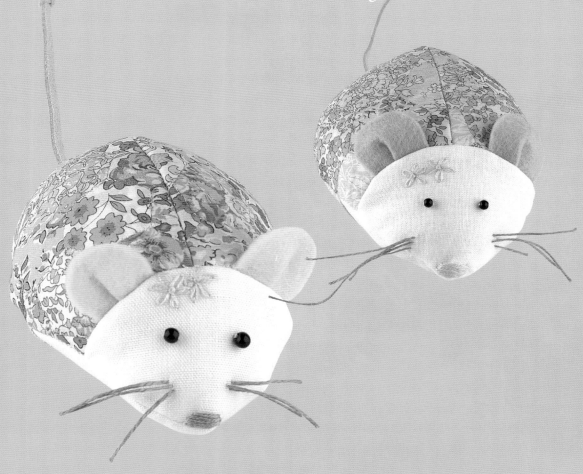

FINISHED MEASUREMENTS
Rosie - Approximately 5"
Lucy - Approximately 4"

Requirements

MUMMY ROSIE

- Thirty-Two ¾″ EPP Hexagon Papers and Perspex Template.
- Thirty-Two 2″ squares of fabrics in assorted prints for the Mouse back/hexagons.
- Mouse Base - 5″ x 6″ Rectangle of neutral fabric.
- Mouse Face - 3″ x 5″ Rectangle of neutral fabric.
- Mouse Ears - 2″ x 3″ Felt.
- Scissor Pocket - 3.5″ x 6″ Print Fabric
- Pellon Fusible Fleece - Two 4″ x 5.5″ Rectangles (iron on the back of the EPP Panels).
- Mouse Tail - 8″ of thin Faux Suede or Ribbon.
- 12″ Waxed floss, Jute Cord or DMC Thread for the Whiskers.
- 2 small back beads for the eyes (4mm Black Pearl).
- Small Embroidery Scissors - 2.5″.
- Additional 8″ Ribbon to secure the scissors.

MISS LUCY

- Forty-four ½″ EPP Hexagon Papers and Perspex Template.
- Forty-four 1.5″ squares of fabrics in assorted prints for the Mouse back/hexagons.
- Mouse Base - 4″ x 5″ Rectangle of neutral fabric.
- Mouse Face - 2.5″ x 4″ Rectangle of neutral fabric.
- Mouse Ears - 1.5″ x 2.5″ Felt.
- Scissor Pocket - 3.5″ x 6″ Print Fabric.
- Pellon Fusible Fleece - Two 3″ x 5″ Rectangles (iron on the back of the EPP Panels).
- Mouse Tail - 6″ of thin Faux Suede or Ribbon.
- 12″ Waxed floss, Jute Cord or DMC Thread for the Whiskers.
- 2 small back beads for the eyes (4mm Black Pearl).
- Small Embroidery Scissors - 2.5″.
- Additional 8″ Ribbon to secure the scissors.

FOR BOTH MUMMY ROSIE AND MISS LUCY

- Your preferred Pincushion stuffing.
- DMC Floss 962 (Dusty Pink) for the Nose.
- DMC Floss 605 (Pink), 225 (Soft Pink) and 828 (Light Blue) for Hand Quilting and Embroidered Flowers.

TIP: If you are using thin or white fabrics for the Mouse face and Base you may also want to back it with some PELLON.

INSTRUCTIONS

1 Trace or photocopy the Mouse pattern pieces from the template pages and cut around the shapes ready for use.

2 Prepare the thirty-two ¾″ hexagons for Rosie or forty-four, ½″ hexagons for Lucy ready for English Paper Piecing. Please refer to the "English Paper Piecing" in the Techniques section. Sew together two sections of hexagons so the pieced panels are large enough to cover the 'Back' pattern piece prepared in step 1.

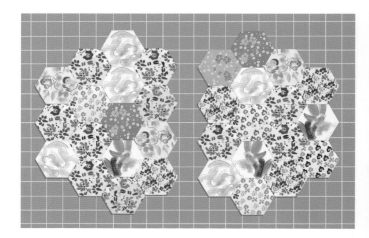

Pictured are the two panels for Rosie.

3 With a warm iron gently press the two panels. Remove your papers and gently iron again. To the back of each panel, iron on one of the Pellon rectangles, ensuring that the adhesive side is facing the back of your hexagons. Take care around the exposed area and the bottom of your iron.

4 From each EPP panel cut one "Back" Piece, ensuring one is cut in reverse. Place a pin in the panel to mark the "centre back seam". Take to your sewing machine and using a small stitch, sew ⅛″ inside the cut line to secure your hexagons and prevent your hand stitches from becoming unstitched.

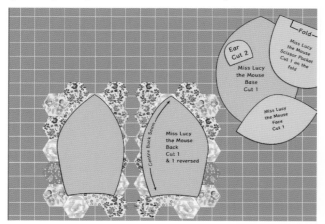

5 Using your pattern pieces prepared in step 1, cut one Base, one Face and one Scissor pocket from your chosen fabric.

6 Cut Two Ears from felt. Using the fold lines on the pattern piece, fold the felt ears and pin them into position where marked on the head piece. Sew, with your sewing machine, ⅛″ in from the edge to secure. Sew your small bead eyes into place now.

7 Sew together the two back pieces along the centre seam. Tack your tail into place approx. ⅛" inside the edge at the back where the seams join.

8 Pin the head to the back along the curve ensuring that your mouse ears are tucked back. Sew together with your sewing machine.

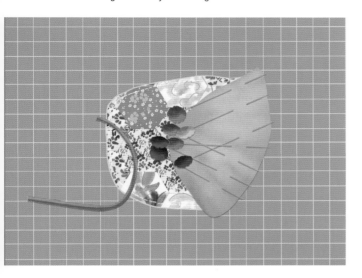

9 For extra detail, hand quilt a couple of the hexagons towards the back of your mouse and add a Lazy Daisy and French knot to the centre of one hexagon. Embroider two lazy daisies with French knots above one eye, near an ear. Refer to "Hand and Embroidery Stitches" in the Techniques Section

10 Fold the Scissor pocket in half, right sides out and with a larger stitch on your sewing machine, sew it into place on the mouse base. Position one end of the ribbon for the scissors into place by tacking it on the side seam near the top of the pocket.

11 Pin your mouse back/head panel to your base, right sides facing and ensuring that your tail and ribbon are out of the way, sew with your sewing machine. Leave a 2 - 3" turning gap at the back, either side of the tail.

12 Turn right side out. Fill with your preferred Pincushion stuffing and hand stitch the opening closed with a Blind Stitch. Refer to "Hand and Embroidery Stitches" in the Techniques section.

13 Thread through your whiskers and trim to length. Trim your tail to the desired length. Take two strands of your DMC Thread and stich a little nose onto your mouse using a Satin stitch. Please refer to "Hand and Embroidery Stitches" in the Techniques Section.

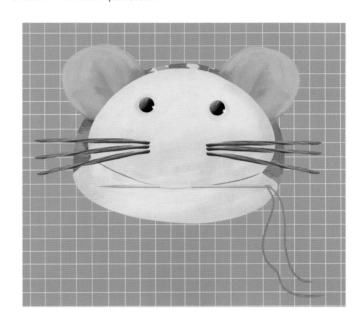

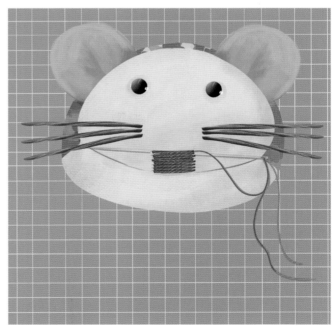

14 Fold a loop at the end of the scissor ribbon, fold it over the handle of the scissors and hand stitch/secure into place. Embellish with a Lazy Daisy - refer "Hand and embroidery Stitches" in the techniques section. Your mouse Pincushion is now ready to use.

Pretty Clamshell Tissue Cover

Adding that extra touch of handmade your handbag, a nappy bag, your car or to add to the Towel Gift Set, you are guaranteed to have the best-looking Tissues in town.

Requirements

- Twenty-eight 2" Clamshell papers and Template
- Twenty-eight 2.5" squares or an assortment of scraps for the clamshells
- Three 12" x 4" Natural Linen for the base and top of the clamshells
- One 11 ¾" 8" Pink print fabrics for the lining
- 16" length of Cotton Trim
- 8" x 10.5" Pellon Fusible Fleece
- DMC Thread in 225 Soft Pink
- One packet of Medium Travel Tissues
- Sewing Machine

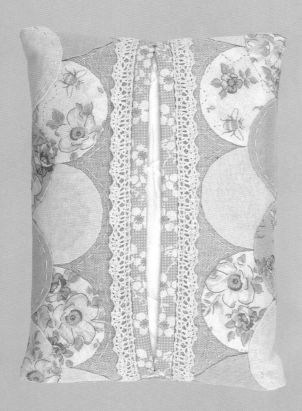

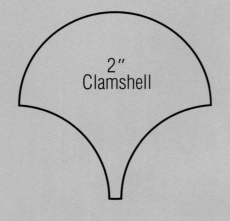

2"
Clamshell

INSTRUCTIONS

1 Prepare the 28 Clamshells ready for English Paper Piecing. Please refer to English Paper Piecing – Preparing shapes with curves" in the Techniques section.

2 Take two of the 12" x 4" natural linen rectangles and along the 12" edge, press a fold 1.5" up from the edge with your iron.

3 Divide the clamshells into two groups of 14. Lay each group into three rows - five clamshells in the top row, four clamshells in the second row and five clamshells in the third row. Play with the layout until you are happy with the placement.

4 Please refer to English Paper Piecing and Joining the Pieces – Clamshells in the Techniques section and join your clamshells into rows and begin to applique the clamshells to the linen.

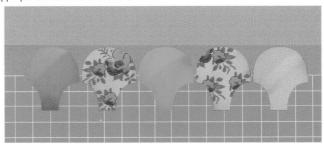

5 Once you have appliqued the third row on each panel, remove all the remaining papers and gently press with your iron.

6 With your rotary cutter, trim off the bottom of the clamshells on both panels at the point where the curves of the Clamshell finish and begins to curve inwards to form the 'tail'.

7 Trim both panels back to an overall height of 3 ¾".

8 With your sewing machine, sew one clamshell panel to each 12" side of the remaining 12" x 4" Linen panel ensuring that the clamshells face out from each other.

9 With your rotary cutter, trim the panel back to 8" x 10" ensuring that the 8" is the length of the clamshell side of the panel and the 10" is the overall length across the clamshells and center linen panel.

10 Following the manufacturer's instructions, iron the Pellon to the back of the trimmed panel.

11 Using DMC Thread 225 in a soft pink, hand quilt along the top curves of the clamshells, each side of the center linen panel and along some of the clamshells as pictured.

12 Place the lining and the pieced panel right sides facing and with your sewing machine, sew along both 8" sides. Please note that your lining is ¾" longer than the pieced panel.

13 Turn right sides facing out and press. Your lining fabric will form a contrast edge.

14 Cut the Cotton trim in half to form two 8" lengths. With your sewing machine or by hand, sew one piece of the Cotton trim to each of the 8" ends.

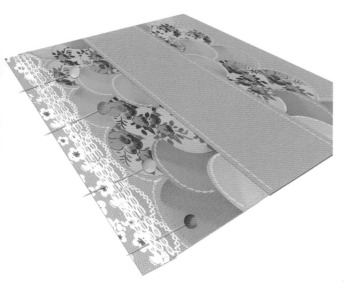

15 With the exterior of the tissue cover facing up, fold both ends in so that they meet in the middle. Pin into place and with your sewing machine, sew both ends closed.

16 Using a Whip stitch, see "Hand and Embroidery Stitches" in the Techniques section, sew each end of the center opening closed approximately 1".

17 Turn your Tissue holder right sides facing out.

18 With DMC Thread 225 sew a 'Cross Stitch' to each end of the opening. This will help to reinforce the whip stitch from Step 16.

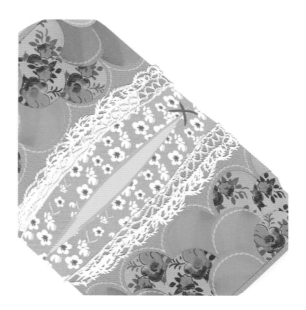

19 Remove the packaging from the tissues and slide the tissues into your new handmade cover. They are now ready to be gifted or added to your handbag, nappy bag or car.

Pretty Little Flower Tape Measure Cover

I love to have pretty things around me when I sew and every now and then I like to sew with tiny shapes. This cute little Tape Measure cover will give you a chance to play with some small hexagons without committing to a large project and make something pretty in the process.

FINISHED MEASUREMENTS
Approximately 3" diameter

Requirements

- Eight ¼" Hexagon Papers
- Two ½" Hexagon Papers (for the tab at the end of the Tape Measure)
- Small scraps of fabrics for the Hexagons
- Two 5" Square of fabric for the top and bottom
- One 12" x 4" rectangle of fabric for the side (Please see steps 9, 10 and 11 to confirm)
- 12" Cotton Lace
- Retractable Tape Measure
- DMC 962 (Dusty Pink) and 828 (Light Blue) 165 (Green)
- Cardboard or 160 – 220gsm cardstock

INSTRUCTIONS

1 Position your Retractable Tape Measure on the cardstock and trace the circumference of the tape measure taking care to stay close to the edge of the tape measure to ensure a snug fit of your cover. Repeat this so that you have two circles. Cut the circles out with your scissors and set aside. There is a circle on the template page for the Tape Measure that I used.

2 Prepare your eight ¼" hexagons ready for English Paper Piecing. Please note that for the ¼" hexagons you will require a slightly smaller seam allowance because of their size. Sew together your Hexagon flower. Leave your papers in. Set aside. Refer to "English Paper Piecing" in the Techniques Section.

3 With a Whip Stitch, applique a ¼" hexagon to a scrap of fabric that you want to use for the tab on the end of your tape measure (Refer to "Hand and Embroidery Stitches" and "Applique" in the techniques section). On this occasion, leave the paper in. Once the ¼" hexagon is sewn to the fabric you can then centre the ½" EPP Paper (or template) on top and cut your fabric for the ½" hexagon. Ensure you add the seam allowance if you are using the EPP Paper.

4 Continue to prepare both your ½" hexagons and set aside.

5 Applique your Hexagon flower onto your selected fabric for the cover top, leaving the papers in.

6 Refer to the "Hand and Embroidery Stitches" in the Techniques section and using the Lazy Daisy, French Knot and Running stitch, embellish around your hexagon flower. Gently press with a warm iron.

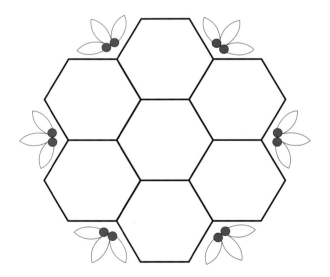

7 Lay your Hexagon Flower top right side facing down and centre one of the cardstock circles on top and trim the fabric ½" bigger all around the circle. Glue baste the circle of fabric to the cardstock as if basting an EPP Shape/curve. Gently press with a warm iron.

8 With the second cardstock circle, repeat step 7, this time using your selected fabric for the base.

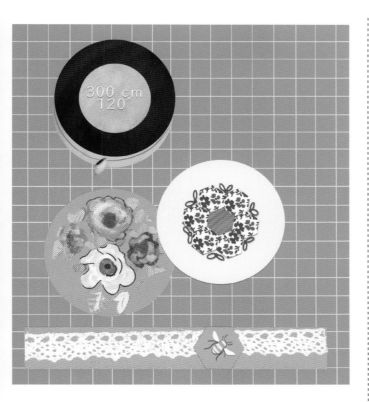

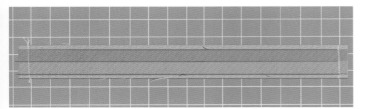

15 Place your top and side strip right sides facing and whip stitch around the circle, joining the two pieces. The short ends of the rectangle need to finish close to each other.

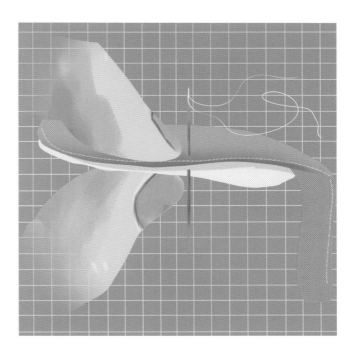

9 Using your retractable tape measure, measure around one of the circles for either the top or bottom of your cover to get your circumference of your circle. Add ½″ and this will become your measurement (x).

10 Measure the width of your tape measure. Multiply this by two and add ½″. This will be your measurement (y).

11 Cut out a rectangle of fabric that measures (x) by (y)

12 Fold the rectangle in half along the long sides, right sides facing and with your sewing machine, sew the long side of the strip together. Stopping in the middle of this length leaving a 2″ – 3″ turning gap. Press the seam open.

13 Sew each end closed and then clip the corners. Turn the rectangle unit right sides out and press again.

14 Optional - Trim the lace to your measurement (x) from Step 9 and using a running stitch, or a sewing machine, sew the length of cotton lace to the long strip folding the short ends to the back side of the strip and sew into place. The ends of the trim will now be sewn on the inside of your tape measure cover. Add any other embellishments you like. One option is to add a fussy cut hexagon to the side.

16 Remove the paper from the top circle and turn the unit right side out.

17 Whip stitch your base into place. When you get approximately half way around place your retractable tape measure inside, ensuring that the button to retract your tape measure is facing upwards and the tape is at the opening. Continue to whip stitch the gap closed. I have left the bottom paper in but you could remove it if that is your preference.

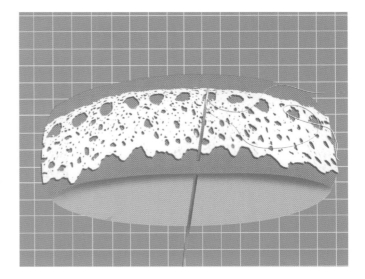

18 Using a whip stitch, face your two ½″ hexagons wrong sides facing (paper still in place) and sew three sides together. Now slide in the metal end of the tape measure and continue to sew your hexagons closed. Your needle will go through the tape measure so you can continue to close the gap. Your tape measure is now pretty and ready to use.

Spring Time
Embroidery
Organiser

Functional and pretty. A sweet little organiser to help keep your embroidery project and supplies in the one spot. Ready to grab as you leave home so that you will be ready to take a few moments out of your day to add a stitch or two.

FINISHED MEASUREMENTS
Folded 7" x 7" / Open 7" x 19"

Requirements

- Eight 2″ Hexagon Papers and Template
- Four 2″ Half Hexagon Papers and Template
- Seven 1″ Scallop Papers and Template
- One 1″ hexagon paper

OUTSIDE OF THE ORGANISER

- 7″ x 4″ Cream Fabric (Embroidery background)
- 7″ x 2.5″ rectangle light blue fabric
- Various fabrics for the 2″ full and half hexagons and the 1″ Scallops
- 19.5″ x 7″ rectangle of Pellon fusible fleece

INSIDE POCKETS

(Left Hand Section)
- One 5.5″ x 7″ rectangle feature fabric
- One 3.5″ x 7″ clear Vinyl
- One 2″ x 7″ rectangle pink floral fabric (binding strip)

(Middle Section)
- One 7″ x 7.5″ floral fabric
- One 9.5″ x 7.5″ Cream fabric (top Pocket)
- One 6.5″ x 7.5″ rectangle Pink fabric (middle pocket)
- One 3.5″ x 7.5″ pink floral fabric (bottom pocket)
- Three 7.5″ lengths cotton lace or ribbon

(Right Hand Section)
- One 7″ x 7.5″ rectangle pink floral
- One 6.5″ x 7.5″ rectangle cream floral (Pocket)
- One 1.75″ x 3.5″ rectangle cream felt
- One 7.5″ length of cotton lace or ribbon
- One 3″ square cream fabric for the hexagon embroidery
- One 2″ square of Pellon fusible fleece to back the hexagon embroidery
- One 1″ pearl look button
- 20″ of Cream Ribbon
- 60″ Binding

- DMC Floss BLANC – White, 727 Yellow, 3727 Mauve, 598 Blue, 818 Soft Pink and 3348 Sage Green
- Small Crochet Flower (Optional)
- Leather 'Handmade' tag (Optional)
- Applique Glue
- Millennium Pen
- Binding Clips

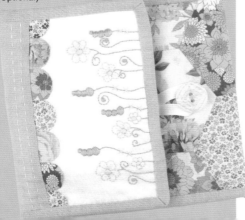

INSTRUCTIONS

1 Prepare the Hexagons, Half Hexagons and Scallops ready for English Paper Piecing and then piece the hexagon panel in 5 columns as pictured. Please refer to 'English Paper Piecing' in the Techniques section.

2 Trim the hexagon EPP Panel back to 14″ x 7″

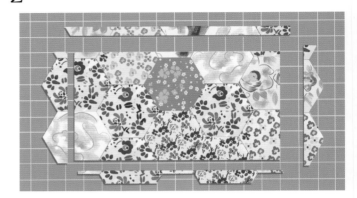

3 Using a light Box, trace the embroidery design onto the 7″ x 4″ rectangle of cream fabric. Trace the smaller flower design onto the centre of the 3″ square of cream fabric. Set aside.

4 English Paper Piece together the seven 1″ scallops along the straight edges. Give them a gentle press with a warm iron to ensure that they lay flat.

5 On the wrong sides of the scallops apply small dots of applique glue along the seam allowance around the curves. Position the Scallops along the top of the traced embroidery panel and press allowing the glue to dry.

6 Applique the scallops into place and then remove the papers.

7 With a sewing machine, sew the 7″ x 2.5″ rectangle of blue fabric along the top of the scallops and then sew the hexagon panel to the other side of the blue fabric creating the outside cover of the organiser.

8 Iron the Pellon to the back of the cover panel as per the manufacturer's instructions. Using the 1″ hexagon paper as a guide, cut a hexagon (no seam allowance) from the 2″ square of Pellon, centre it behind the design traced to the 3″ square of cream fabric (Step 3).

9 Embroider the cover, referring to 'Hand and Embroidery Stitches' in the Techniques Section for the stitch guide.

Use DMC 3727 Mauve and Backstitch to embroider the sprouting swirls, finishing off the ends with a satin stitch.

Use DMC 3348 Sage Green and Backstitch to embroider the remaining flower stems.

Use DMC 727 Yellow and a Satin Stitch and embroider the centre of the flowers and a large cross stitch for the crosses on the stems.

Use DMC 818 Soft Pin and Backstitch to embroider the petals of the flowers.

Use DMC 598 Blue and a satin stitch to embroider each of the four circles on the remaining flowers.

Hand Quilting.

Use DMC BLANC White and add two rows of Hand Quilting / Running stitch above the scallops on the blue fabric.

10 Following the guide above, embroider the design on the 3″ square. Set aside.

INSIDE POCKETS

LEFT HAND SIDE POCKET

11 Take the 2″ x 7″ binding strip and fold both long ends to the centre and press. Fold in half and press again, creating a binding strip that measures ½″ x 7″.

12 Using binding clips, position the binding strip so it covers one of the 7″ sides of the clear vinyl and with a sewing machine, topstitch into place.

13 Lay the vinyl pocket to the left-hand side of the 5.5″ x 7″ rectangle of feature fabric. Use binding clips to hold it in place and with a ⅛″ seam and a longer stitch length on your sewing machine, baste into position.

MIDDLE POCKET

14 Take the 9.5″ x 7.5″ Cream fabric (Top Pocket), 6.5″ x 7.5″ rectangle Pink fabric (middle pocket) and the 3.5″ x 7.5″ pink floral fabric (bottom pocket) and with an iron press each in half, right sides facing out, creating three pockets measuring 4.75″ x 7.5″, 3.25″ x 7.5″ and 1.75″ x 7.5″.

15 With a sewing machine, sew a 7.5″ length of cotton lace or ribbon to the top (fold) of each pocket.

16 Take the 7″ x 7.5″ floral fabric and layer the three pockets on top, lining up the bottoms with the white pocket going first, then the pink, followed by the pink floral. Pin into place and with a ⅛″ seam sew the pockets into place along each side and the bottom.

17 With a water erasable pen, measure in 2.5″ from the side and rule a line down all three pockets. Measure over another 2.5″ (5″ from the edge) and mark another line down the three pockets. Using DMC 818, Soft Pink and a running stitch, sew down the three pockets so that there are now 9 pockets in total. Remove the pen markings.

RIGHT HAND SIDE POCKET

18 Take the 6.5″ x 7.5″ rectangle of cream floral fabric and press in half, right sides facing out to make a 3.25″ x 7.5″ pocket. With a sewing machine, sew a 7.5″ length of cotton lace trip to the top (fold).

19 Measure in 3″ from the left-hand side and with a water erasable pen, mark a vertical line. With a running stitch and DMC 818, soft pink, sew along the line creating two pockets. Remove the pen markings.

20 Take the embroidery made at Step 10 and trim it so that it has a seam allowance all around the Pellon backing. Baste it to the 1″ hexagon and give it a warm iron. Remove the paper and applique the embroidered hexagon to the right-hand side of the pocket. Finish off with some hand quilting around the hexagon using DMC 818, soft pink.

21 Lay the pocket on top of the 7" x 7.5" rectangle of pink floral fabric, pin into place and with a ⅛" seam allowance, sew the pocket into place.

22 Using a running stitch and DMC 727 Yellow hand stitch the felt into position by centring it in the space above the pocket.

23 With a sewing machine, sew all three panels together creating the inside of the organiser.

24 Optional. If you are adding a Handmade Tag or a Crochet flower, sew them into position now. Sew a length of ribbon under the crochet flower to be used to secure embroidery scissors.

25 Lay the organiser cover and inside wrong sides facing and pin together. With a sewing machine, sew around the entire outside of the organiser using a ⅛" seam allowance.

26 Sew along the seam lines between the three internal panels to secure the cover and lining.

27 Sew the button to the back cover as pictured.

28 Fold the organiser closed and measure a length of ribbon that will go from the left-hand side of the organiser, around the button and back. It will be approx. 5" - 5 ½" depending on the exact position of the button. Pin and secure into place using a ⅛" seam allowance.

29 Sew the binding to the inside of the Organiser, mitring the corners as you go. Please refer to 'Binding' in the Techniques Section for more information.

30 Using binding clips, fold the binding to the front, hand stitch into place and you are finished.

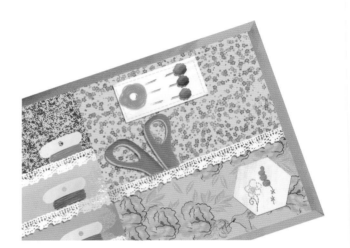

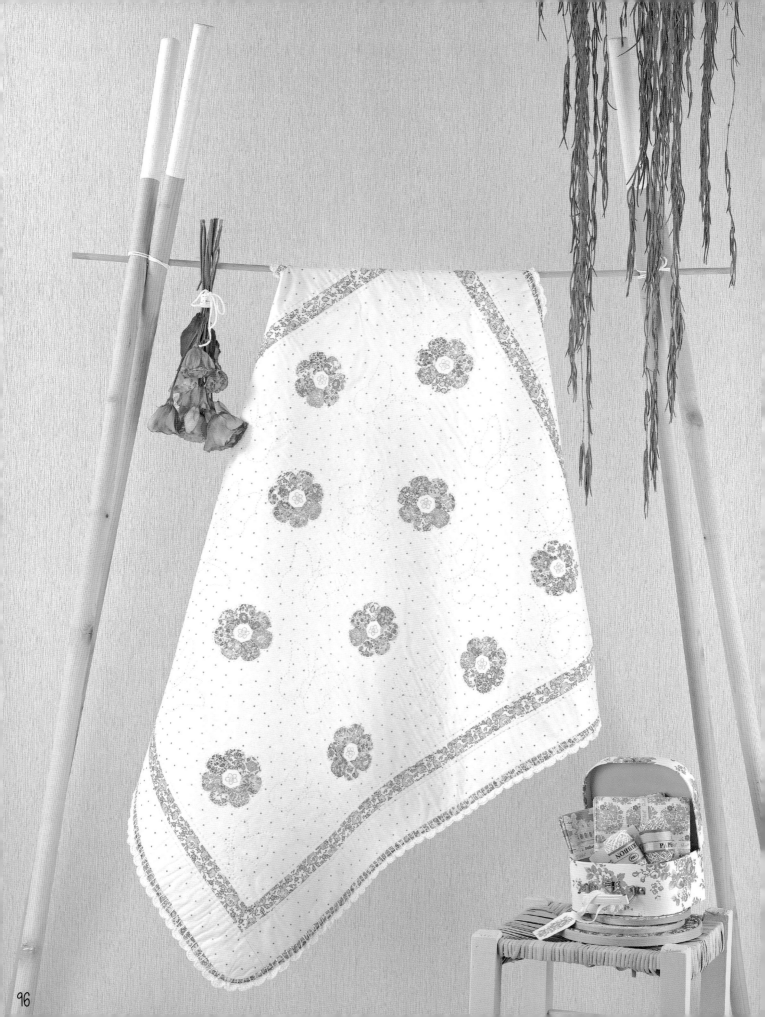

Sweet Daisy Baby Quilt

Welcoming a new baby into a family is always a special occasion and this Sweet Daisy Baby Quilt can become your next family heirloom. Stitched with love as you piece the Daisies and then finish the project by adding the hand quilting and an optional sweet crochet edge. This sweet project allows you to use some of your small Liberty/fabric Scraps.

FINISHED MEASUREMENTS
35" x 40"

Requirements

🪡 Twelve EPP Heptagon Papers*

🪡 Eighty-Four EPP Flower Petal Papers*

*Please note that the Heptagon and petals are a custom shapes/sizes created for this project. Please see the note on 'custom shapes' in the English Paper Piecing Techniques section.

🪡 Eighty-Four 2" squares of complimenting Liberty Prints for the daisy petals.

🪡 Centre Panel – 28" x 33" of a Gold Swiss dot on Cream fabric

🪡 10" Square of 'off white' fabric for daisy centres.

🪡 First Border (Liberty) Two 28" x 1.5"

              Two 35" x 1.5"

🪡 Outer Border Four 35" x 3" – Gold Swiss Dot on Cream fabric

🪡 160" length of binding to compliment the Liberty Border.

🪡 Template Plastic

🪡 40" x 45" piece of Backing Fabric

🪡 40" x 45" piece of batting

🪡 ¼" quilters Tape

🪡 Millennium Pen to transfer the Embroidery design.

🪡 Water Soluble Pen for marking Quilting Design

🪡 DMC Floss 605 (Pink) Embroidered Flowers

🪡 DMC Floss 727 (Yellow) Embroidered Flower Centres

🪡 DMC Perle 8 Thread, Colour 818 (Soft Pink) for hand quilting

🪡 DMC Natura Cotton – one 50g Ball in Ibiza (white)

🪡 Crochet Hook (size 3)

INSTRUCTIONS

1 Prepare your Heptagon and Petal papers by tracing or copying onto 160gsm card and cutting out.

2 Using a Millennium Pen (or your preferred pen) trace out the centre embroidery design found in the template section, 12 times onto the 10" square of off white fabric ensuring that they are spaced out enough that you can later cut your Heptagons with the seam allowance and not have them overlapping.

3 Embroider the Daisy flowers as follows:

         Using DMC 605 (Pink) stitch the Daisy petals in a backstitch.

         Using DMC 727 (Yellow) stitch a Satin Stitch for the centre of the daisy.

         Refer to "Hand and Embroidery Stitches" in the Techniques section for the stitch guide.

4 Refer to the "English Paper Piecing" in the Techniques section – Creating a Template. Make a template of your Heptagon from Template plastic.

5 Centre your heptagon template over your embroidered flowers and trace the outline with a water-soluble pen. Cut out your 12 Heptagons.

6 Prepare your Heptagon and Petals ready for English Paper Piecing. Please refer to "English Paper Piecing" in the Techniques section. With the petals, you will need to baste the entire shape, not just the curve like you would with a clamshell.

7 Sort your petals into groups of seven and add a heptagon to each pile. Tip. These groupings can be stored together with a binding clip until you are ready to sew.

8 English Paper Piece your flowers together creating 12 daisy flowers. Please refer to the "English Paper Piecing – Joining the pieces" in the Techniques Section. These flowers can be sewn the same as a hexagon flower. When completed, give them a gentle press with your iron, removing the heptagon paper but leaving the petals papers in place and set aside.

ASSEMBLING YOUR TOP

9 With your sewing machine take the centre 28" (Top) x 33" (Side) panel and add the first border by sewing a 28" x 1.5" strip to each 28" side using a ¼" seam allowance. Press with your Iron. Sew a 35" x 1.5" strip to each 35" side completing the first border. Press with your Iron.

10 Add your second border by sewing a 35" x 3" strip to each of the 35" sides. Press with your iron. Sew a 35" x 3" strip to each of the two remaining sides and press with your iron.

11 With your iron, gently press fold marks into the centre panel of your top as pictured. Start by folding your top in half vertically and press. Then fold in the two sides creating quarters. Repeat by folding your top in half horizontally and gently press being careful not to press out your previous folds. Repeat by folding the top and bottom section in thirds.

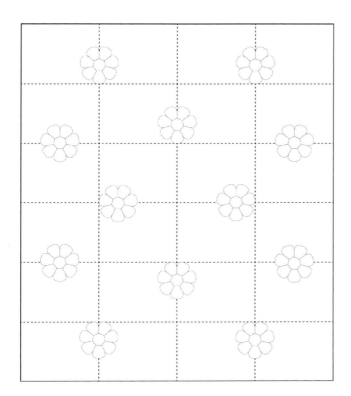

QUILTING

15 Trace the two butterflies found in the templates section onto your template plastic with a pencil. Cut out along the outline of the shapes so they are ready to use as a quilting template.

16 Make a quilt sandwich - refer to Quilt Sandwich in the Patchwork and Quilting techniques section.

12 Use the fold marks for the guide of placement of your Daisy flowers. Lay your flowers in a pleasing manner and when you are happy with their position, turn your daisies over so the back side is facing up and apply a few dots of Applique glue to the outer seam allowance on the back of your Daisies. Turn the daisies back over and position them into place. Apply a little pressure and allow the glue to dry. Repeat for all 12 daisies.

13 Applique your daisies into place using a blind stitch - Refer to "Hand and Embroidery Stitches" in the Techniques section.

14 Once your flowers are appliqued into place, flip your work over so the back side is facing up. Carefully cut away the backing fabric as pictured, leaving approximately ½" seam allowance INSIDE the applique stitching line all around. Remove your papers. Press with your Iron. For more details on this step please refer to "My Preferred Applique Method" in the Techniques Section.

17 Using a DMC Perle 8 Thread, hand quilt your project - refer to Hand Quilting in the Patchwork and Quilting Techniques Section. I hand quilted around each Daisy as well as ¼" each side of the first border.

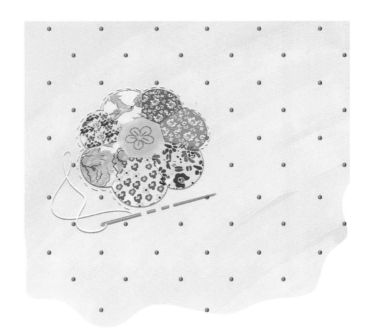

18 Using your butterfly templates made in step 15 and a water-soluble pen, trace the butterflies in the open spaces, adding in the extra details of the wings and body. Hand quilt the butterflies.

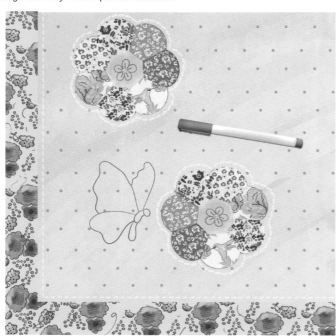

19 Optional. Round off each corner by placing a cup or saucer at the corner and mark the curve. Carefully trim the corners so they are rounded.

20 Bind your quilt. – See Binding in the Techniques section.

OPTIONAL - ADDING A CROCHET EDGE – (US TERMS)

21 Using a knitters needle and a long piece of yarn, run the needle up under the back side of the quilts binding up through to the centre of the binding. Pull the yarn all the way through securing the knot under the binding. Referring to "Blanket Stitch" in the "Hand and Embroidery Stitches" in the Techniques Section, add a blanket stitch all the way around your baby quilt finishing off back where you started. Spacing the stitches at approximately ¼" - ⅜" apart, knotting your yarn and burying the yarn end.

22 Slip stitch into your first space and then chain 2 to start your first scallop.

23 Complete Five Double Crochet (dc) next to the first stitch (with your 2 chain this will count as a 6 dc).

24 Single Crochet (sc) into the next open blanket stitch space.

25 Moving onto the next blanket stitch space, complete 6 Double Crochet (dc)

26 Repeat steps 24 and 25, working your way around your blanket until you are back where you started.

27 Slip stitch to finish and bury your thread.

May your new finish wrap a precious new baby in love.

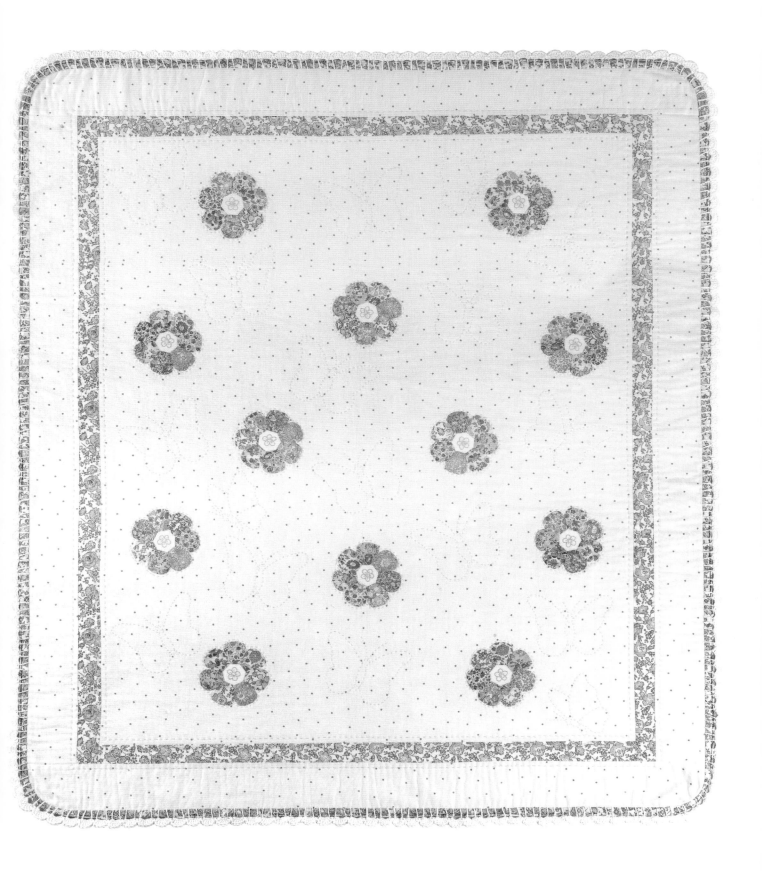

Tea Time Placemats

It doesn't matter if it is for a lazy Sunday brunch or a special Afternoon Tea with a loved one, a table setting that is pretty and has a little handmade always makes me happy.

FINISHED MEASUREMENTS
12" x 18"

Requirements (for one placemat)

- Twelve 4" Quarter Circle papers
- Twenty-Three 2" square papers
- Three Fat 8ths of fabric for the 2" squares
- One Fat 8th of a check fabric
- 13" x 19" Background Fabric
- 13" x 19" Backing Fabric
- 13" x 19" of Batting or Parlan
- 70" of a 2" Wide Binding
- 65" of a thin Cotton Lace
- DMC Floss BLANC (White) for Hand Quilting
- Sewing Machine

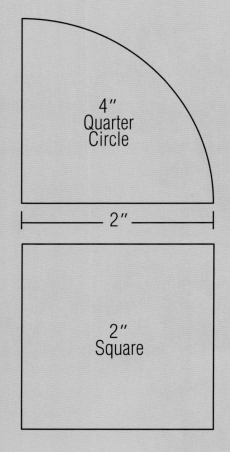

4"
Quarter
Circle

2"

2"
Square

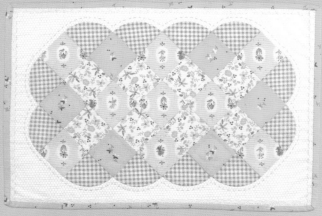

INSTRUCTIONS

1 Prepare your Squares and quarter circles ready for English Paper piecing. Please refer to the "English Paper Piecing Basics" section. The quarter circles will need to be basted around the entire shape. This project is also a good one to play with some fussy cutting to highlight an element within a fabric.

2 Lay your prepared shapes out and play with placement. Once you are happy with the layout, English Paper Piece you're your panel. Please refer to the "English Paper Piecing – Joining the Pieces" in the Techniques section. For this project, it is easier to piece rows first and then join the rows together until you have your full panel.

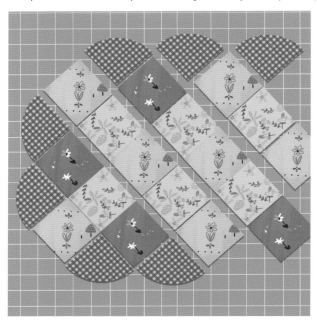

3 With your iron, gently press your work and remove all the papers excluding the ones on the outer edge.

4 Fold your Background rectangle into quarters and place a pin at the folds so you have reference points to centre your English Paper Pieced Panel. Lay right side up on your work surface.

5 On the back of your English Paper Pieced panel apply small dots of Applique glue to the seam allowance on the outer edge all the way around.

6 Flip the English Paper Pieced panel back over and centre it onto the background fabric using your pins as reference to help centre it and press down. Allow the glue to dry.

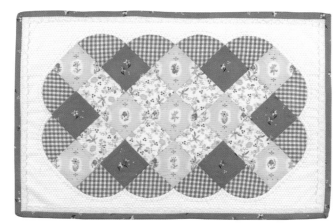

7 Applique your panel onto the background using a Blind stitch - Refer to "Hand and Embroidery Stitches" in the Techniques section.

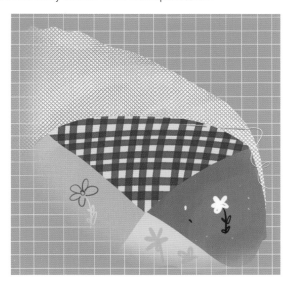

8 Flip your completed panel over so that the back side is facing up. Carefully cut away the backing fabric only, leaving approximately ½" seam allowance all around the inside of the sewn line. Remove all remaining papers and press. For more information on this please see "My Preferred Applique Method" for when I am working with an English Paper Pieced panel like this, in the Techniques Section.

9 With a Rotary Cutter and Ruler trim your placemat back to 12" x 18".

10 Make a quilt Sandwich – refer to Quilt Sandwich in the "Patchwork and Quilting" techniques section.

11 Quilt as desired. I Hand Quilted ¼" all around the outside of the English Paper Pieced panel, and on 8 of the 2" squares. Please refer to the "Patchwork and Quilting" techniques section.

12 With your sewing machine, sew the cotton lace to the outside of the placemat, positioning it just under ¼" in from the edge so that when you sew your binding to your project it will just be caught under the binding. Start by sewing along the top. When you get to the end trim off your cotton lace and start the next side, working your way around your placement.

13 Attach your binding. Please refer to "Binding" in the Patchwork and Quilting Techniques section. Your placemat is now ready to use.

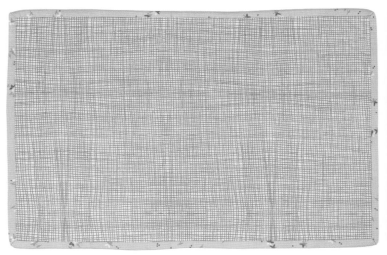

Reverse of placemats

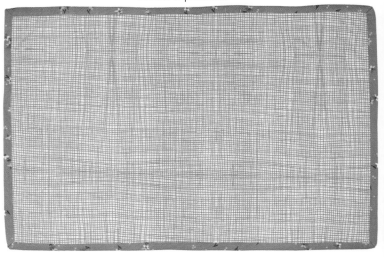

THE
Bumblebee
COLLECTION

Tilda®

Tenderness Pincushion

You can never have enough pincushions but what makes this one special is the optional removable bowl that can store the other items that you like to keep handy whilst you sew.

The sides of the bowl can be folded down to reveal the embroidery or left up to hold larger items like spools of thread. The bowl is also great for holding binding clips, bobbins of thread, EPP glue sticks, refills etc.

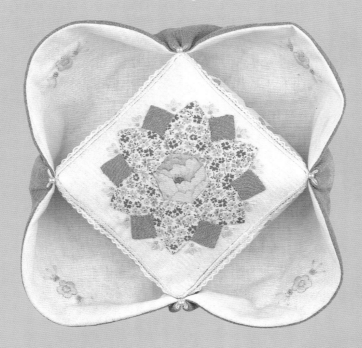

FINISHED MEASUREMENTS
Pincushion 5"
With bowl is approximately 7"

Requirements

PINCUSHION

- One Tenderness Hexagon paper *
- Six Tenderness Petal papers *
- Six Tenderness leaf papers *
- Two 4" square papers
- Four 1.5" x 4" Rectangle papers

*Please note that the Tenderness Flower shapes above are custom shapes. Please read the note on "Custom Shapes" in the English Paper Piecing Techniques Section.

- 6" square of Floral fabric for the flower petals
- 5" square of Pink fabric for the leaves
- 2" square of Pink for the Hexagon Centre
- 6" square of cream fabric for the flower background
- 6" square of Pellon Fusible fleece
- Four 2" x 4.5" rectangles Floral fabric for the pincushion sides
- One 4.5" square of Pink Fabric for the pincushion base
- 20" cotton lace trim or ribbon
- "Fibrefill" or your preferred Pincushion stuffing.
- DMC Floss 225 Soft Pink, 747 Soft Blue, 3348 Soft Green and 744 Pale Yellow
- Millennium Pen to transfer the Embroidery design.
- Water Erasable Pen

BOWL

- One 11" square of Cream fabric for Bowl lining
- One 11" square of Pink Fabric for Bowl exterior
- One 10" Pellon Fusible Fleece
- Four Buttons or charms for embellishment
- Four Pearl look pins (optional)

INSTRUCTIONS

1 Prepare your Tenderness flower, rectangles and square papers by tracing or copying onto 160gsm card and cut out your flower shapes, rectangles and squares ready for English Paper Piecing. Please refer to "English Paper Piecing" in the Techniques section and see the note on custom shapes in the Techniques section.

To baste your leaf shapes please follow the guide below.

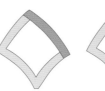

2 Sewing the gentle curves of the flower.

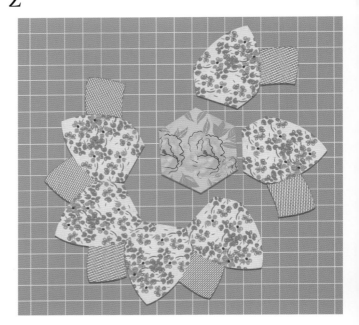

A- To create this flower, you first need to make 6 separate Petal and Leaf Units. When sewing your leaf to your petal face both RST and line up the bottom of the leaf to the start of the curve on the petal. You will see that the bottom part of the leaf will align with the petal. Sew from point A to point B. Secure your stitch.

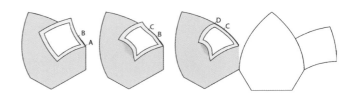

B- Place your index finger between the petal and leaf, gently bend the leaf over your index finger and line up the leaf edge with the petal edge and continue to sew remembering to secure your stitch as you go. Don't be scared to bend your papers to make the edges come together. Make 6 petal and leaf units.

C- Once you have made your 6 petal and leaf units you can then join these units together by facing two unit's right sides facing and sew the straight sides first (point A to point B) ensuring that you secure your stitch at point B.

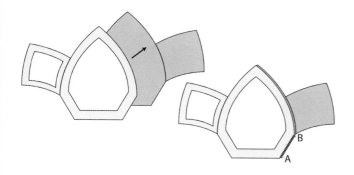

Then proceed to sew the curves applying the same method at (a), securing your stitch as you go to ensure a nice tight stitch/finish. Continue to join in all 6 units leaving the last seam between the sections open.

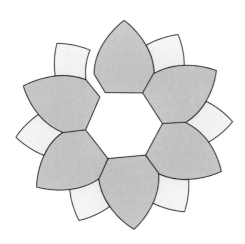

D- Attach your hexagon by starting at either end of the internal petal ring. Face the hexagon RST with the base of a petal and start to stitch your way all around the hexagon. When you get to the end and your hexagon is completely sewn in, continue to sew the last two petals together forming your completed flower. Give your flower a gentle press with your iron. You can remove the centre hexagon but leave the remaining papers in.

3 Have your 6″ square of cream background fabric on your workspace, right side facing up. Lay your flower right sides facing down and apply a few dots of Applique glue to the outer seam allowance on the back of your completed flower. Flip the flower over so the right side is facing up and position your flower onto the centre of your 6″ cream square. Apply some pressure by hand or press with an iron and allow the glue to dry.

4 Applique the flower into place using a blind stitch. Please refer to "Hand and Embroidery Stitches" in the Techniques section.

5 Once your flower is appliqued into place, flip your work over so that the back side is facing up. Carefully cut away the backing fabric as pictured, leaving approximately ½″ seam allowance all around. To help make the removing of the papers easier, with your fabric scissors, cut into the petal points, but not too close to the stitched line. Remove all the papers and press with your iron.

6 If you prefer to mark your embroidery to your pincushion top, do it now before ironing the Pellon to the back, otherwise iron the Pellon to the back of your pincushion top.

7 Embroider a 3-petal lazy daisy flower with French knots as pictured around the applique flower. Gently press your work with an iron. Refer "Hand and Embroidery Stitches" in the techniques section.

8 Centring the flower, trim your pincushion top back to 4.5″ square. Baste to a 4″ square EPP paper.

9 Sew your prepared 1.5″ x 4″ rectangles to the sides of your pincushion top. Remove the paper from the top of your pincushion. Sew the sides of the rectangles together.

10 Proceed to sew the bottom square onto the pincushion along three sides. Remove all the papers and turn your pincushion right side out. Stuff with your preferred pincushion stuffing and blind stitch the opening closed. Please refer to "Hand and Embroidery Stitches" in the Techniques section.

11 Hand stitch the cotton lace or embroidery trim around the top of your pincushion using a blind stitch.

OPTIONAL BOWL

12 Cut two 10.5″ circles from the 11″ fabric squares that you have chosen for the bowl.

13 Cut one 9.75″ circle from the Pellon.

14 With a water erasable pen, transfer all the markings found on the template page onto the fabric that you are using for the inside of your bowl including the embroidery design.

15 Iron (no steam) the Pellon to the back of the above ensuring that it is centred. The Pellon is cut smaller so that it will not be included in the seam allowance and thus reducing bulk.

16 Embroider the floral design using DMC 225 Soft Pink and Satin Stitch for the flower petals and DMC 744 Pale Yellow and Satin stitch for the centre of the flower. Use DMC 747 Soft Blue for the lazy daisy stitches and DMC 3348 Green for the French knots. Please refer to "Hand and Embroidery Stitches" in the techniques section. Once completed gently press with an iron.

17 Face both bowl fabrics right sides together and with your sewing machine, sew around the entire circle with a ¼″ seam allowance leaving a 3″ gap for turning.

18 Turn right side out and slip stitch the opening closed. Press with your iron.

19 Pleat where the lines indicate and stitch into place by hand. Add a button or charm for embellishment.

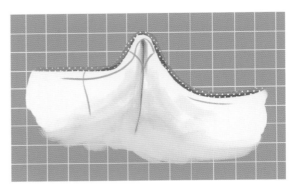

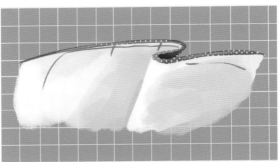

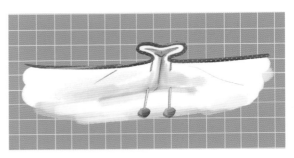

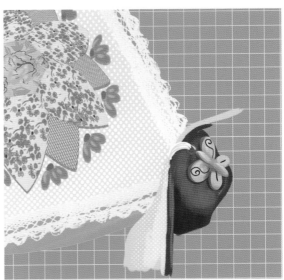

20 The 'bowl' can be either hand sewn to the corners of your pincushion securing into place permanently or alternatively use 4 pearl headed pins one at each corner to hold into place by pushing in the pins to catch both the pleat of the bowl and the corners of the pincushion.

Together
we make a
Family

Together We Make a Family Mini Quilt

A simple sentiment that can sometimes be lost in today's world. So, what better way to display it in your home for that gentle reminder to all x

FINISHED MEASUREMENTS

12" x 12.5"

Requirements

- Eight Pointed Dresden papers *
- Eight Rounded Dresden papers *
- Fabric for the Dresden's. If fussy Cutting you will need to ensure you have eight repeats to achieve the same look as pictured.
- 13" Square of Cream Background Fabric
- 13" square of Pellon Fusible Fleece
- 13" Background Fabric
- 5" x 3" rectangle for hanging sleeve
- 52" soft pink piping
- 52" Picot Edge Binding
- DMC Embroidery Floss in: - 312 Dark Blue, 747 Light Blue, 151 Candy Pink, 819 Soft Pink, 166 Sage Green, 165 Soft Green
- Millennium Pen
- Light Box
- Embroidery Hoop (Optional)
- Mini Quilt Frame
- Sewing Machine

*Please note that the Dresden's are a custom size of this existing shape. Please read the note on "Custom Shapes" in the English Paper Piecing Techniques section

INSTRUCTIONS

1 Prepare the Pointed and Rounded Dresden papers by tracing or copying the shapes from the template pages onto card and cut out your papers ready for English Paper Piecing. Please refer to "English Paper Piecing" in the Techniques section. If you wish to make your own Templates for these custom shapes please refer to "Creating a Template" in the Techniques Section.

2 English Paper Piece the Dresden's together forming a circle by alternating the pointed and rounded Dresden's. Gently press with an iron.

3 Fold the background square into quarters and gently press with an iron to mark the quarters.

4 Centre the Dresden ring on the background using the ironed quarter marks as a guide. Fold half of the ring back and apply small dots of glue along the seam allowance around the outer and inner edge of the Dresdens, NOT along the sewn seams.

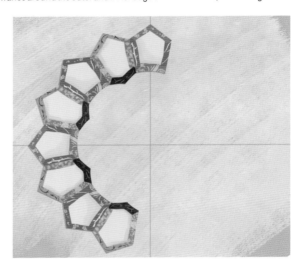

5 Fold back and press, allowing the glue to dry. Repeat for the other half of the Dresden ring.

6 Using a coordinating thread, applique the Dresden ring into place on both the outer and inner edges using a Blind stitch. Refer to Hand and Embroidery Stitches in the Techniques Section.

7 With your fabric sheers, carefully cut into the background fabric that is behind the Dresdens leaving a good ¼" allowance away from the sewn line. With a smaller pair of scissors, snip into the fabric at the points to assist with removal of the papers. For more information on this please see "My Preferred Applique Method" in the Techniques section.

8 Remove the papers and gently press.

9 Using a light box and a Millennium Pen, trace the embroidery design into the centre of the Dresden ring. When tracing the Lazy Daisy petals, only transfer over the dots.

10 Following the manufactures instructions, iron the Pellon, or your preferred embroidery stabiliser to the back of the panel. I prefer to use the Pellon as it acts as a batting for my finished project and helps to hide my stitches from showing through from the back of my embroidery work.

11 Embroider the design as follows. Refer to "Hand and Embroidery Stitches" in the Techniques section as a reference for the stitches used. If you prefer to use a hoop when embroidering, place your panel into your hoop and stitch the following:

Using DMC 151 (Candy Pink) stitch "Together we make a" in Backstitch and the petals for the large flower at the bottom in Satin Stitch.

Using DMC 312 (Dark Blue) stitch "Family" in Backstitch along the edge of the letters and then going back in using more backstitch stitches to fill the space.

Using DMC 166 (Sage Green) stitch the small leaves in a Satin Stitch and the vines in Backstitch.

Using DMC 819 (Soft Pink) stitch the petals for the medium flower in Satin Stitch.

TIP: To soften the look of Lazy Daisy stiches and French Knots you may prefer to remove your work from the hoop for the last two colours.

Using DMC 747 (Light Blue) stitch the small flower petals with a Lazy Daisy stitch.

Using DMC 165 (Soft Green) add the French knots to the centre of the light blue flowers and fill the centre of the light and darker pink flowers with French knots.

OPTIONAL HANGING SLEEVE

15 Take the 5″ x 3″ rectangle for the Hanging sleeve and fold over both 3″ ends ¼″ and topstitch with your sewing machine.

16 With a Rotary Cutter, cut the rectangle in half making two 1.5″ x 4.5″ rectangles.

17 Fold in half lengthways, wrong sides facing and press.

18 On the back, at the top of your Mini Quilt position a hanging sleeve approx. 1.5″ in from the left side and pin into place. Repeat this for the right side. With your sewing machine, sew into place with a scant ¼″ seam.

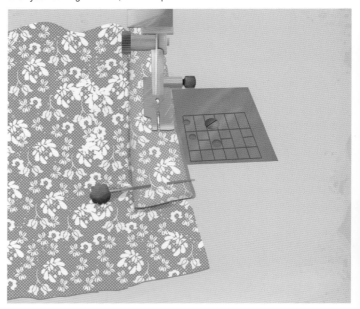

12 Layer your quilt ready for quilting. I have machine stitched inside the centre of the Dresden's and again on the outside of the Dresden's.

13 With your Rotary Cutter and patchwork Ruler, trim the panel back to 12″ wide and 12.5″ in length.

14 Place the Zipper foot on your sewing machine and sew the soft pink piping, one side at a time to the Mini Quilt using a ¼″ seam. Trim and repeat for the next side. Be careful not to stretch the piping as you sew it to the mini quilt.

19 Bind your mini quilt. See "Binding" in the Techniques Section. Place it onto your Mini Quilt frame and Enjoy.

Vintage Dreams Cushion

Bring a renewed life to some vintage linens. They may be your grandmothers or some you have found at a local thrift shop. Add some of your favourite pretty florals and a little hand embroidery and you have the prefect cushion to add a touch of times past to your home.

FINISHED MEASUREMENTS

18"

Requirements

- Seven 1.5" Hexagon Papers and Template
- Forty-Two 1.5" 6-point Diamond papers and Template
- Forty-Two 1.5" Equilateral Triangle papers and Template
- Eleven 3" hexagon papers
- Two 3" half hexagon papers
- Vintage or repurposed Doilies for the 1.5" hexagons
- Seven 5" squares of a variety of florals
- A selection of low volume fabrics for the backgrounds. You can also repurpose the plain linen that can be left after you have cut your hexagon centres.
- Two (2) - 10.25" x 18.5" rectangles for cushion back
- Two (2) - 2" x 4" rectangles for the Zip Tabs.
- 20" square of Pellon Fusible Fleece
- 45 cm Zip
- Size 18 Cushion Insert
- DMC Floss in 3348 Green, 744 Yellow, 818 Soft Pink, 962 Dark Pink
- DMC Perle 8 Thread in ECRU
- 80" of 2" wide binding
- Millennium Pen
- Light Box
- Sewing Machine
- Zipper Foot

INSTRUCTIONS

1 Prepare all your papers ready for English Paper Piecing. Please refer to "English Paper Piecing" in the Techniques section.

2 Cut one of the 3" hexagons into quarters.

3 Using a 1.5" Hexagon Template, Fussy cut your vintage linens so that you have seven (7) 1.5" hexagons for the centre of your larger pieced hexagon units. Please refer to "Cutting your EPP Shapes from Fabric / Fussy Cutting" in the Techniques section.

4 Referring to "English Paper Piecing" in the Techniques section, piece your 7 larger 3" Hexagon units together. Each 3" hexagon unit is made from one 1 ½" Hexagon from the repurposed vintage linen, six 1.5" triangles in florals and six 1.5" 6-point diamonds in low volume fabrics.

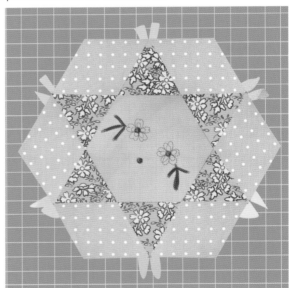

5 Once you have your seven units sewn, lay them out in a pleasing manner and proceed to sew them together adding the 3" half hexagons, 3" full hexagons and the quarter hexagon units around the outer edge of the panel to create the cushion front. This will be trimmed back later for the cushion front.

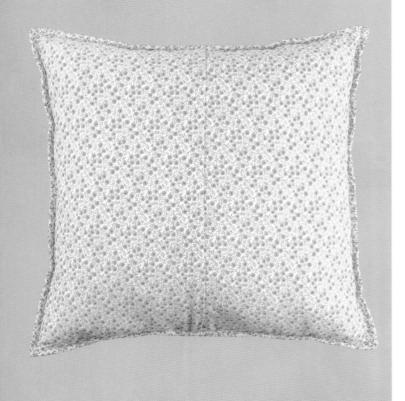

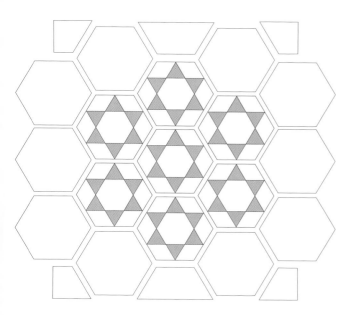

6 Using a light box, trace the embroidery design around your cushion - Two at the top, one to each side and two to the bottom. Please see the templates section for the design. You will be trimming the cushion panel back to 18″ square after quilting so please be careful with the placement of the embroidery designs at the side of the cushion panel to ensure that the embroidery sits within the width of the cushion and does not get lost in the binding. When transferring over the Lazy Daisy from the template page only copy the dots.

7 Following the manufactures instructions, iron the 20″ square of Pellon to the back of your panel being careful not to let your iron touch the adhesive side of the Pellon.

8 Embroider the flower design as follows:

Using DMC 744 (Yellow) stitch the lazy daisy in in the centre of the flower.

Using DMC 962 (Darker Pink) stitch a 'long and short stitch' at the outer edge of the flower petals.

Using DMC 818 (Soft Pink) stitch a 'long and short stitch' to fill in the space between the darker pink and the yellow lazy daisy.

Using DMC 3348 (Green) stitch the green vine using a Split stitch.

Using DMC 818 (Soft Pink) stitch a partial lazy daisy (4 petals) for the flower at the end of the vine.

Using DMC 962 (Darker Pink) stitch two French knots for the flowers at the end of the vine.

Repeat for all six embroideries around the cushion.

Refer to the "Hand and Embroidery stitches" in the Techniques Section for the stitch guide.

9 Using a DMC Perle 8 Thread, hand quilt your project. Refer to Hand Quilting in the Patchwork and Quilting Techniques section. I hand quilted around the outer edge of the seven feature star hexagons as well as the low volume hexagons that forms around the centre star hexagon and then added a lazy daisy to the centre.

10 With a rotary cutter and ruler trim your cushion panel back to 18.5″ square, centring your seven feature star hexagons.

11 Optional - Add a line of hand quilting ½″ in from the edge of your cushion. Once your cushion is bound this line of quilting will sit ¼″ in from the binding. Set aside.

CUSHION BACK – CONCEALED ZIP

12 Remove the metal tab at the end of your zip and with your sewing machine, zigzag the end closed. (This is an optional step but it is something that I like to do to avoid any extra bulk and it eliminates the chance of accidently hitting the needle on your machine against the metal tab, causing damage.)

13 To attach a tab to each end of your zip take your two 2″ x 4″ rectangles and iron them in half making two 2″ x 2″ squares. Open and press two ends to the centre making a rectangle.

14 Lay one rectangle right side up and place the zip on top as pictured. Fold the tab over encasing the end and pin into place. With your sewing machine, top stitch into place.

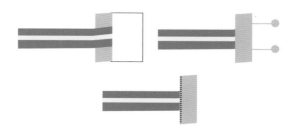

15 Add the second tab to the other end of your zip ensuring that the overall length of your zip with the tabs is at least 18.5″. We will trim away any excess later.

16 With your sewing machine, Zig Zag one of the long 18.5″ sides on each cushion back piece.

17 Fold the zig zag edge under ½″ and press.
Repeat for the other but this time fold under 1″ and press.

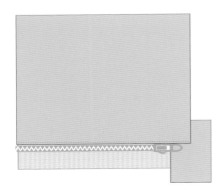

18 Take the cushion back piece with the narrow ½″ fold and using pins, secure the zip into place. Using a Zip foot on your sewing machine, sew into place removing the pins as you go.

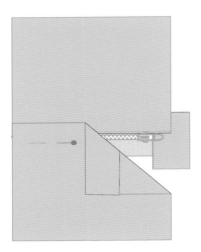

19 Position the other backing piece with the wider 1″ fold over the zip so that the two back pieces overlap just under ½″. Secure with pins and again with the zipper foot on your machine, sew into place removing the pins as you go.
You now have your concealed zip cushion back. Trim away any excess at the tabs.

20 Lay your cushion front and cushion back, right sides facing out, pin and sew into place using a scant ¼″ seam allowance.

21 Bind your cushion. Refer to "Binding" in the Patchwork and Quilting Techniques section.

22 Fill with an 18″ Cushion insert and you have your finished project.

Vintage Pouch

Whether it be a vintage doily from your Great Grandmother or a special find from a local thrift shop it is always nice to repurpose a special treasure. I have a small collection of vintage doilies and tablecloths, many with small stains.

FINISHED MEASUREMENTS

Approximately 5.5" x 6"

Requirements

☙ Twenty-Two 1″ Hexagon Papers and Perspex Template

☙ Twenty-Two 2.5″ Squares in various Low Volume Fabrics for the Hexagons

☙ One 6.5″ Square for the pouch Back

☙ Two 7″ x 8″ Rectangles for the lining

☙ 8.5″ x 8″ Pellon Fusible Fleece (Optional - to fuse onto the back of your hexagon Panel)

☙ Vintage or repurposed Doily (Optional)

☙ Two 20″ lengths of Suede Thonging (commonly found in the Jewellery section of a craft supplies store). You could also use ribbon or cording.

☙ DMC Floss in 962 (Dusty Pink), 828 (Soft Blue)

INSTRUCTIONS

1 Trace or photocopy the Vintage Pouch template pieces and cut around the outside line ready for use.

2 Prepare your twenty-two 1″ hexagons ready for English Paper Piecing. Please refer to "English Paper Piecing" in the Techniques section.

3 Sew together your English Paper Pieced Panel in 5 columns, alternating four hexagons in the first column, five in the second, four in the third etc.

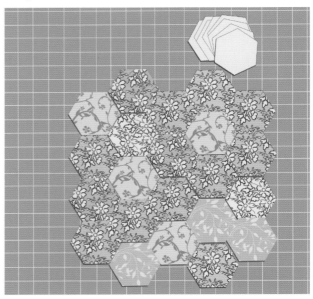

4 Gently press with a warm iron and then remove all the papers.

5 Optional – Iron on a piece of Pellon to the back side of your panel ensuring that the fusible side is facing the back of your panel, not your ironing board. Please see my note on Pellon in the "Essential Tools Section" to help you decide if this step is necessary for you.

6 Take your Vintage Pouch Template and fold down the top section to the "Pouch Exterior" line. Position it over your EPP Panel, pin into place and then cut out your Pouch.

7 Take your cut panel piece to your sewing machine. Set your stitch length to a shorter stitch, (I use a 1.8 stitch length) and sew ⅛th of an inch inside the cut line. This will help secure your hand sewing and stop it from coming unstitched.

8 Hand Quilt or embellish as desired. I have hand quilted one hexagon on the bottom right side and stitched a Lazy Daisy into the centre and added two French knots using DMC Floss in 962 (Dusty Pink) and 828 (Soft Blue). Please refer to "Hand and Embroidery Stitches" in the Techniques Section.

9 OPTIONAL - To add a Vintage Doily. Trim a Doily or vintage linen to fit the pouch. Centre it across the top straight edge of your English Paper Pieced panel, and with your sewing machine, sew into place ⅛" from the top. Then with your sewing machine sew just inside the lace edge around the doily to secure into position.

10 From your 6.5" Square fabric cut out your Vintage Pouch Exterior for the back of your pouch.

11 Place your two Vintage Pouch exteriors right sides together and pin. With your sewing machine, sew from the top right hand side, down and around the curve and back to the other side. Leave the top open. Clip the seam allowance around the curve ensuring that you do not clip into the sewn line. Turn right side out.

12 Unfold the top of your template and from the two 7" x 8" Rectangles cut out your two Vintage Pouch Lining pieces.

13 Lay your two linings right sides together and pin. Mark with a pin, 1" down from the top on both the left and right-hand side. Sew from these points down and around leaving the top 1" open.

14 Approximately 1¼" down from the top (¼" under where you started sewing your side seam), snip into the seam allowance, this will allow the seam allowance above to be folded back. Do not snip all the way into the sewn line. Fold back the seam allowance on the top 1" on both sides and with your sewing machine, sew these sections into place.

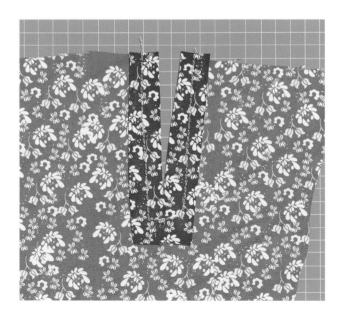

15 Leaving your lining right sides facing in, slide it into the Vintage Pouch exterior, lining up the side seams. Your exterior and your lining will both be wrong sides facing. Your lining will sit 1" taller than your exterior.

16 Fold the lining down ½" towards the top of the exterior of your pouch. Now fold the remaining ½" over again so it sits over the top of your Pouch exterior by approximately ½". Do this for both the front and back of your pouch, ensuring that the side openings line up with the side seams of your pouch. This forms your drawstring casing.

17 With your sewing machine, stitch close to the bottom edge your drawstring casing all the way around.

18 From the left-hand side, feed one piece of your Suede through the front drawstring casing, out through the right and then back through the back casing making one large loop. Repeat for the other piece of Suede but this time from the right-hand side, through the front casing, around through the back casing and out the right forming another loop. Tie each end and trim and excess.

Your pouch is ready to be used.

With Love
Liberty Gift Bag

It is not always possible to make a larger homemade gift but with this cute gift bag you can add that special touch of homemade to any gift. Fill it with Lavender or chocolates, homemade cookies or a special treasure.

FINISHED MEASUREMENTS
7.5" x 10"

Requirements – for one Bag

- Thirty ½" Hexagon papers and Tempate
- Thirty 1.5" squares of various Liberty prints for the heart.
- Two 8" x 9" pieces of linen for bag exterior
- Two 3" x 8" Liberty print for base of bag
- Two 8" x 11.5" cream fabric for lining
- Two 8" x 11.5" Pellon fusible fleece
- One 5" x 6" rectangle of Freezer paper
- Two 8" lengths of Cotton Lace
- 30" of a ½" wide double sided Satin Ribbon
- Complementing DMC Floss

INSTRUCTIONS

1 Prepare the Hexagons for English Paper Piecing. Please refer to "English Paper Piecing Basics" in the Techniques section.

2 Trace the heart from the template pages onto the centre of the Freezer paper and cut out along the drawn line with your paper scissors.

3 Lay your prepared hexagons out in a pleasing manner and English Paper Piece them together forming a panel larger than the heart template. You can use the heart template from step two to ensure your panel is large enough.

4 Iron the freezer paper to the back side of ONE of the 8" x 9" exterior linen pieces, with the heart centred and 1.5" up from the bottom.

5 Cut out the inner heart shape ¼" to ½" smaller than the heart shape of the freezer paper.

6 Cut slits to within a couple of threads of the edge of the freezer paper heart and then with your iron press back the tabs as pictured. Remove the freezer paper.

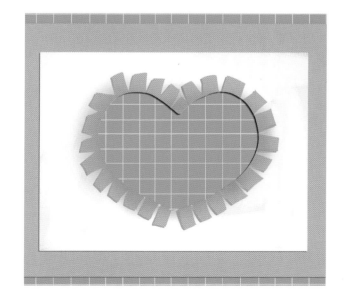

7 On your work surface lay the linen heart right sides down so that the tabs are facing up. Apply a small dot of applique glue to each 'tab'. Centre your Hexagon panel over the heart opening. Apply some pressure with your hands whilst the applique glue dries or alternatively gently press with your iron to speed up the drying process. (Please check the manufactures instructions before applying heat from the iron)

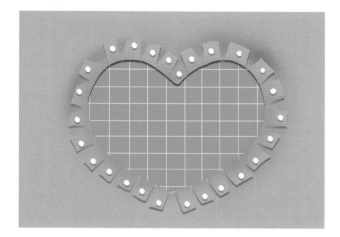

8 Using a Blind Stitch reverse applique your heart. Refer to "Hand and Embroidery Stitches" in the Techniques section,

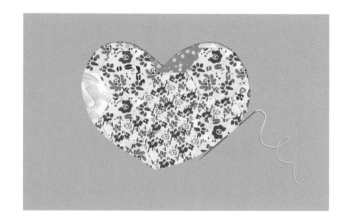

9 With your scissors, trim away the excess hexagon panel from the back of your heart.

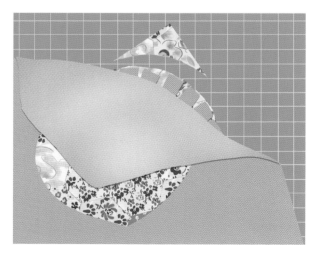

10 With your sewing machine, sew the 3″ x 8″ liberty print fabric to the bottom of the two linen bag exteriors. Press your panels.

11 Following the manufactures instructions, iron the 8″ x 11.5″ pieces of Pellon to the back of the bag exteriors.

12 With your sewing machine, sew the two 8″ lengths of lace trims to the front and back panels of your bag along the seam where the linen and liberty meet.

13 Using a co-ordinating DMC thread and a running stitch, see 'Hand and Embroidery Stitches' in the Techniques section, stitch around the heart and above the lace trim on the exterior bag pieces.

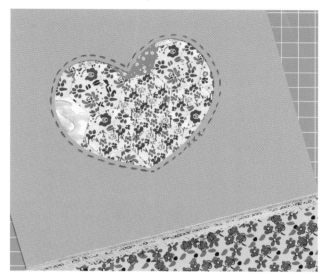

14 Take the 8″ x 11.5″ lining fabric and sew one to the top of each bag exterior with the right sides facing.

15 Open and press with your iron.

16 With both panels open, lay them together, right sides facing. Pin both panels together, lining up the lace and seams. with your sewing machine, sew around the exterior leaving a 3″ turning gap in the lining base.

17 Fold the base corner open so that it lies flat, pin into place. Measure up 1″ from the corner, mark and sew along this line with your sewing machine. With your rotary cutter, carefully trim away the excess. Repeat for both exterior and lining corners.

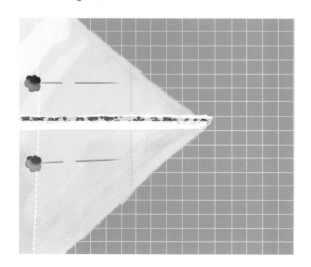

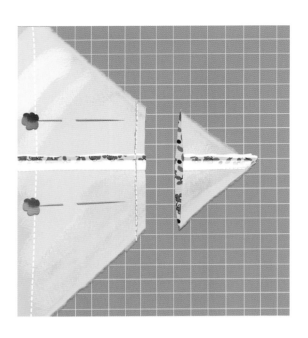

18 Turn your bag right side facing out and slip stitch the opening in the lining closed. Please refer to "Hand and Embroidery Stitches" in the techniques section.

19 With your sewing machine, top stitch around the top of your bag.

20 Find the centre of the length of ribbon and on the back of your bag, centre and pin the ribbon 2″ from the top of the bag. Sew into place by hand or with your sewing machine.

21 Tie a knot in each end of the ribbon and your pretty "With Love Liberty Gift Bag" is ready to fill and gift.

Templates

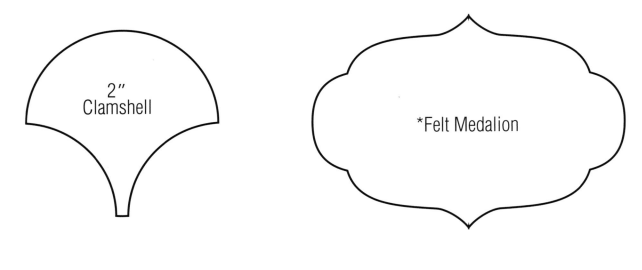

2"
Clamshell

*Felt Medalion

*A Stitch
in Time*

✕ ✕

Text Embroidery Design

1"
Hexagon

1"
Half Hexagon

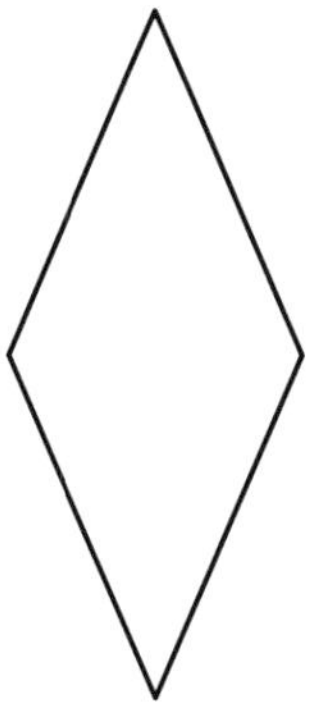

1" 8-Point Diamond

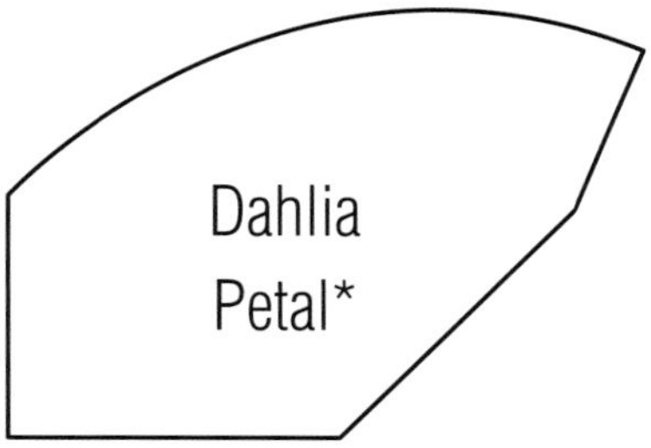

Dahlia
Petal*

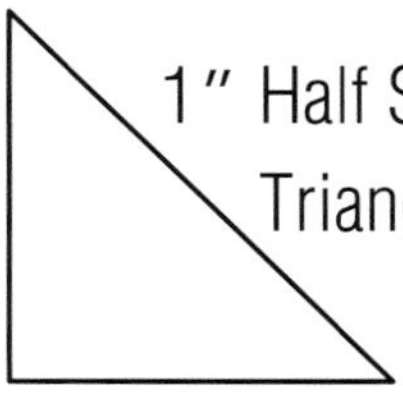

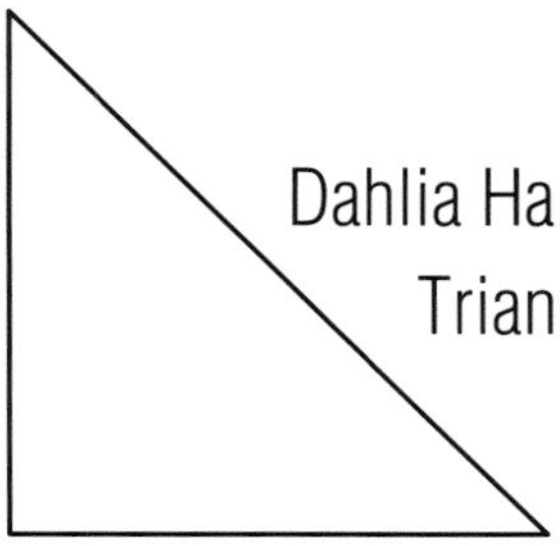

Dahlia Half Square
Triangle*

1" Half Square
Triangle

1" Square

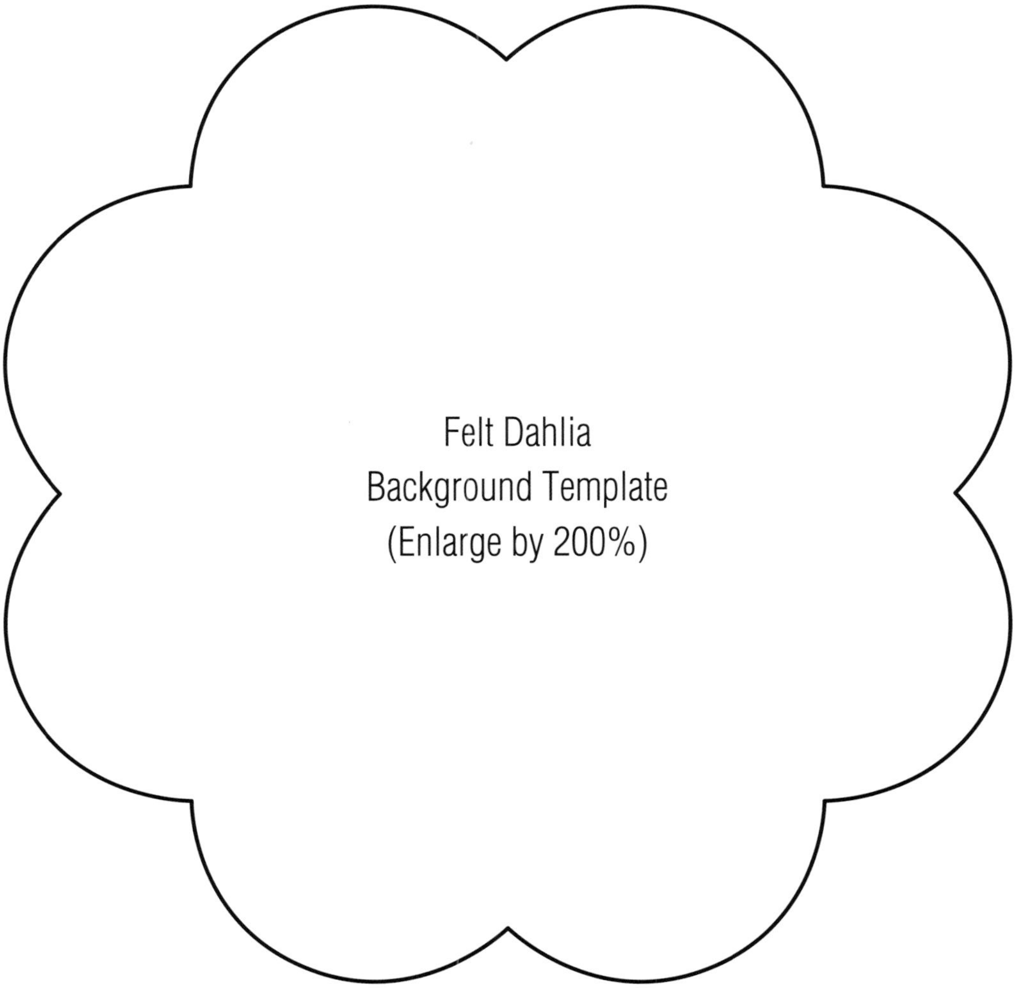

Felt Dahlia
Background Template
(Enlarge by 200%)

Dumpling Bag

Project on Page 54

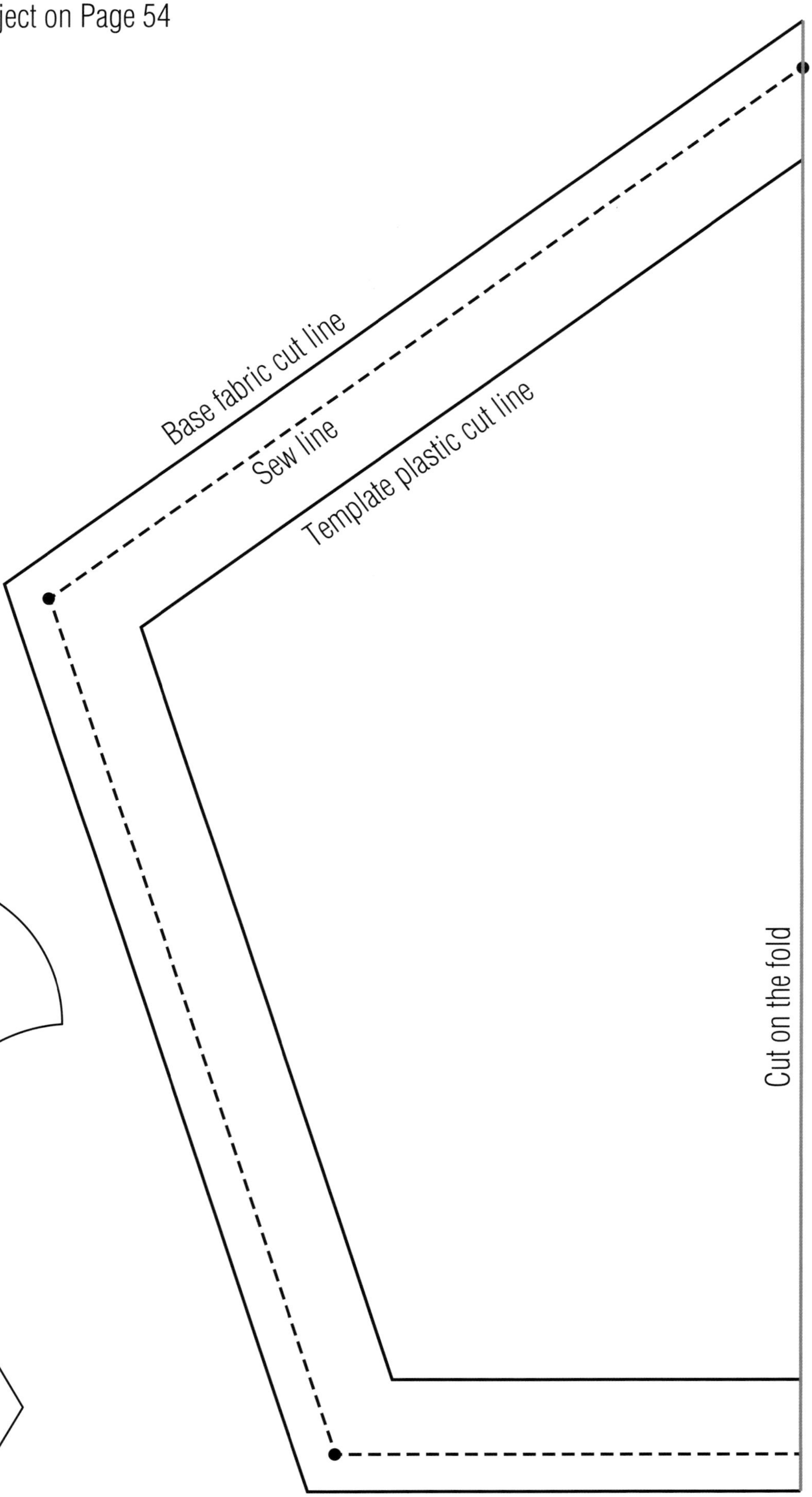
Base fabric cut line
Sew line
Template plastic cut line
Cut on the fold

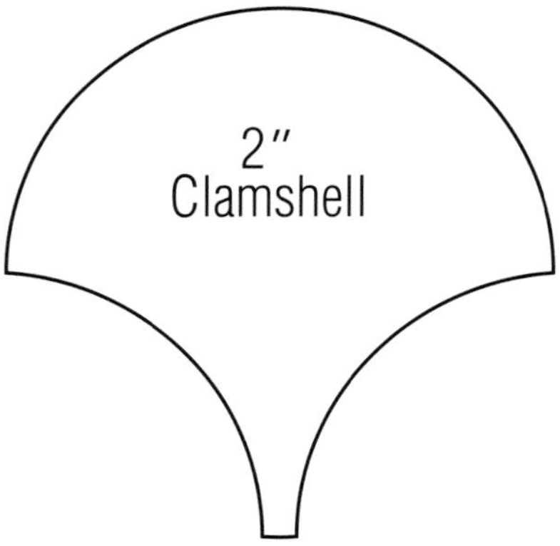
2″
Clamshell

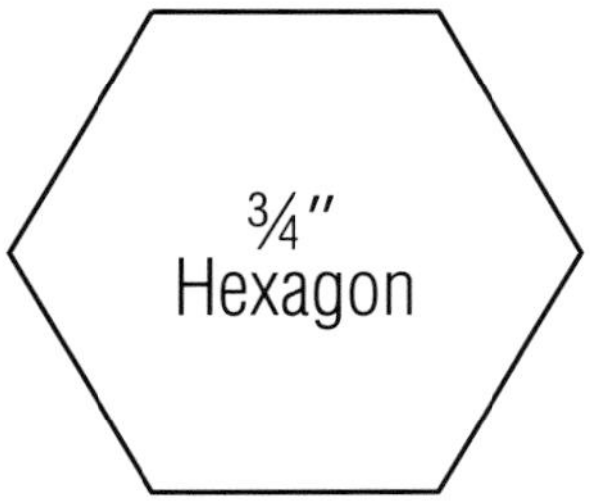
¾″
Hexagon

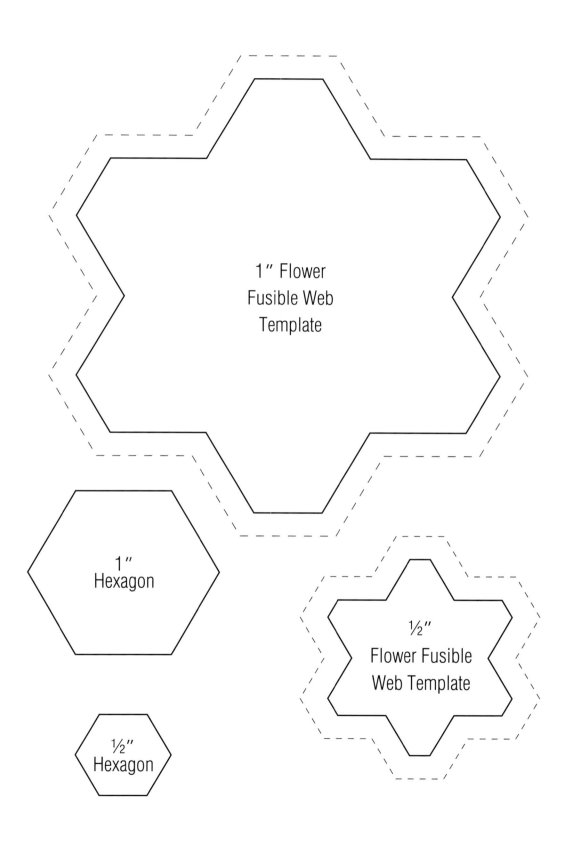

1″ Flower
Fusible Web
Template

1″
Hexagon

½″
Hexagon

½″
Flower Fusible
Web Template

Project on Page 64

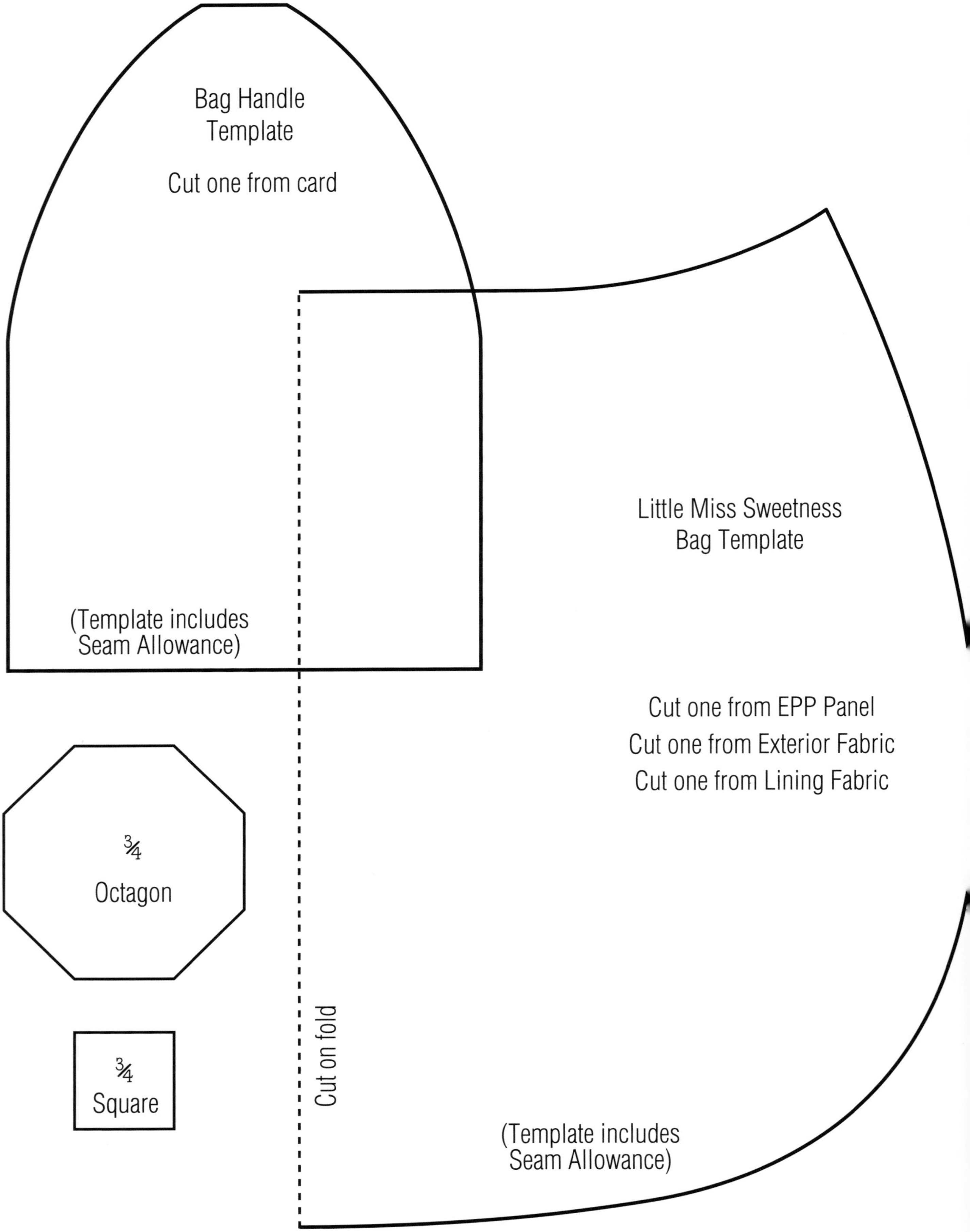

Bag Handle
Template

Cut one from card

(Template includes
Seam Allowance)

Little Miss Sweetness
Bag Template

Cut one from EPP Panel
Cut one from Exterior Fabric
Cut one from Lining Fabric

¾
Octagon

¾
Square

Cut on fold

(Template includes
Seam Allowance)

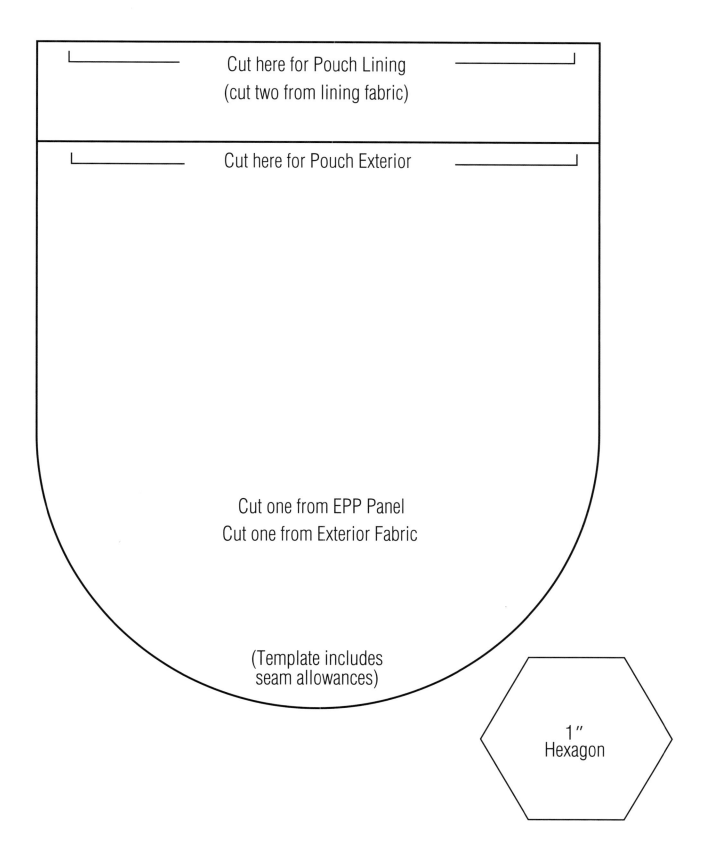

Cut here for Pouch Lining
(cut two from lining fabric)

Cut here for Pouch Exterior

Cut one from EPP Panel
Cut one from Exterior Fabric

(Template includes
seam allowances)

1″
Hexagon

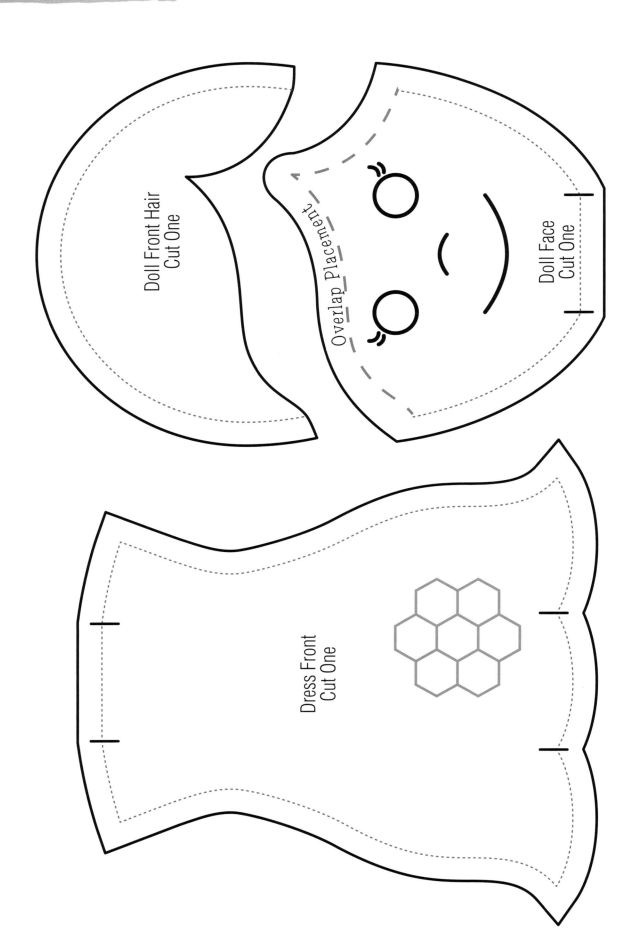

Doll Front Hair
Cut One

Overlap Placement

Doll Face
Cut One

Dress Front
Cut One

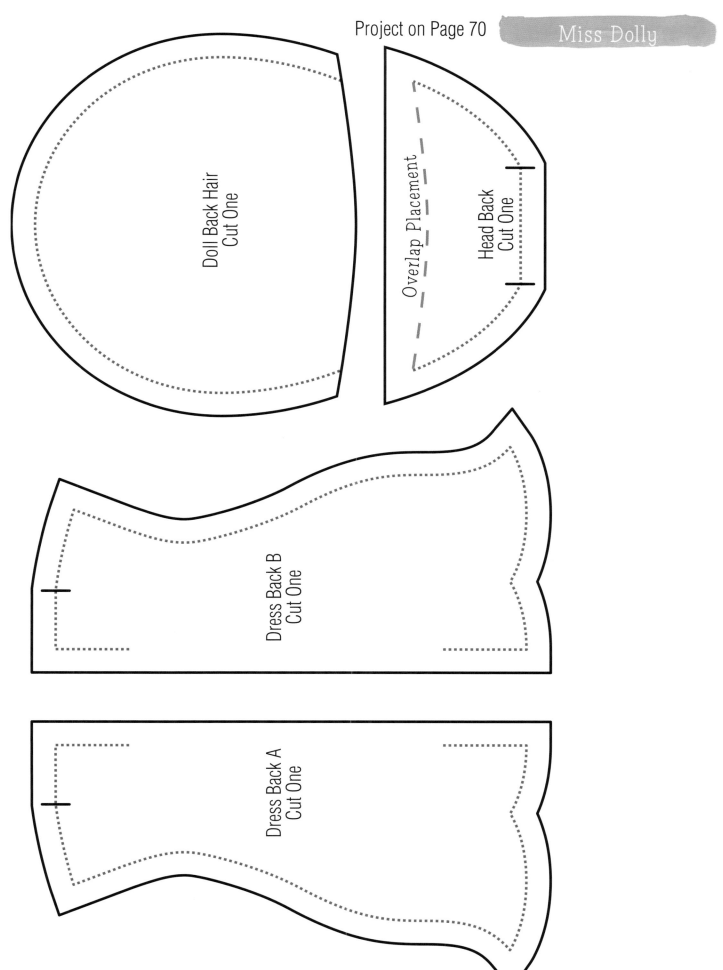

Miss Dolly

Doll Back Hair
Cut One

Overlap Placement

Head Back
Cut One

Dress Back B
Cut One

Dress Back A
Cut One

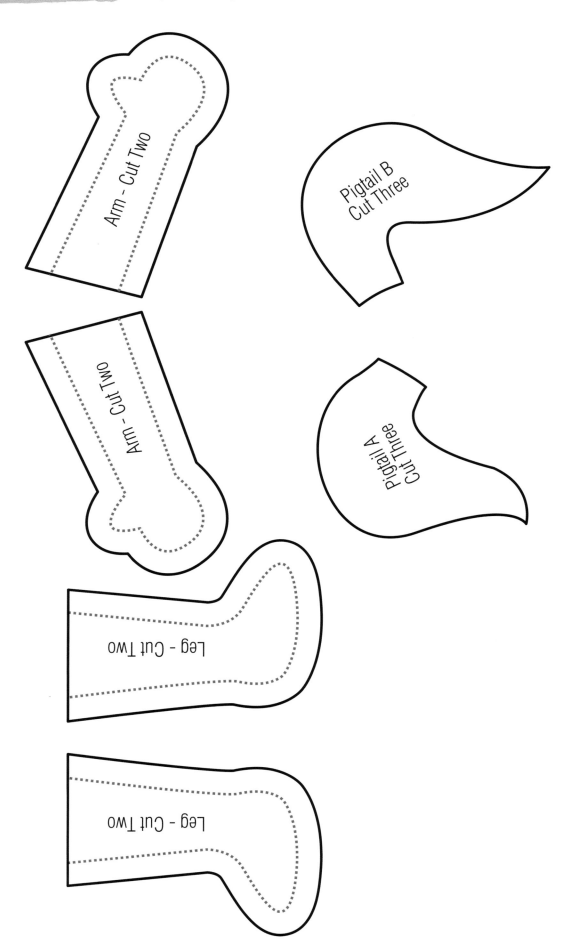

Arm – Cut Two

Pigtail B
Cut Three

Arm – Cut Two

Pigtail A
Cut Three

Leg – Cut Two

Leg – Cut Two

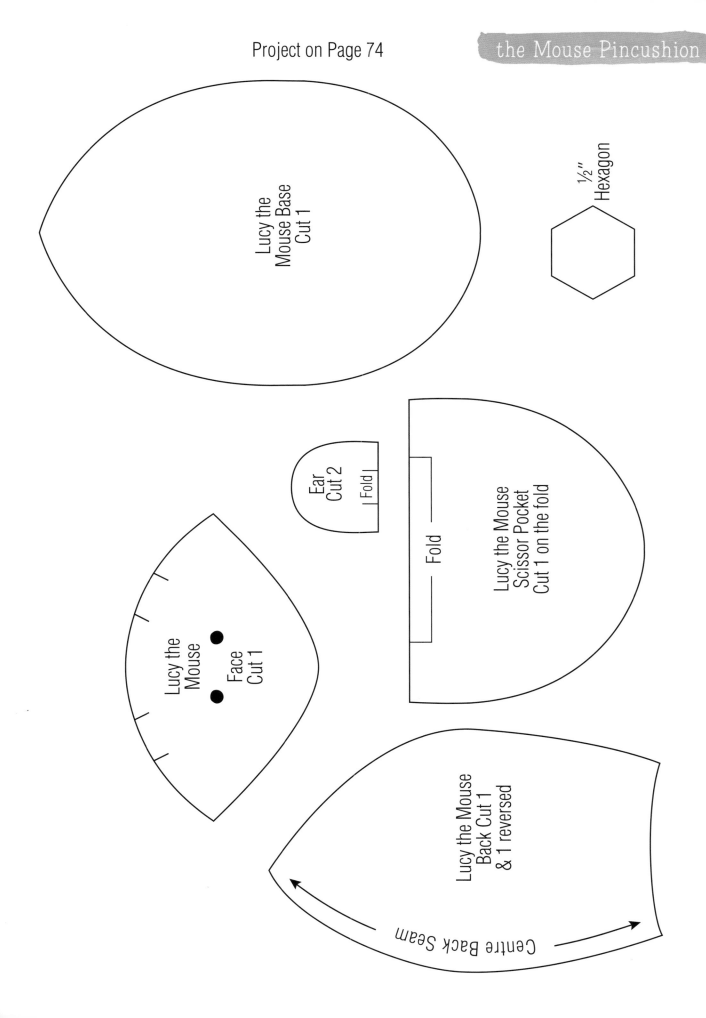

Lucy the
Mouse Base
Cut 1

½"
Hexagon

Ear
Cut 2
Fold

Lucy the Mouse
Scissor Pocket
Cut 1 on the fold

Fold

Lucy the
Mouse

Face
Cut 1

Lucy the Mouse
Back Cut 1
& 1 reversed

Centre Back Seam

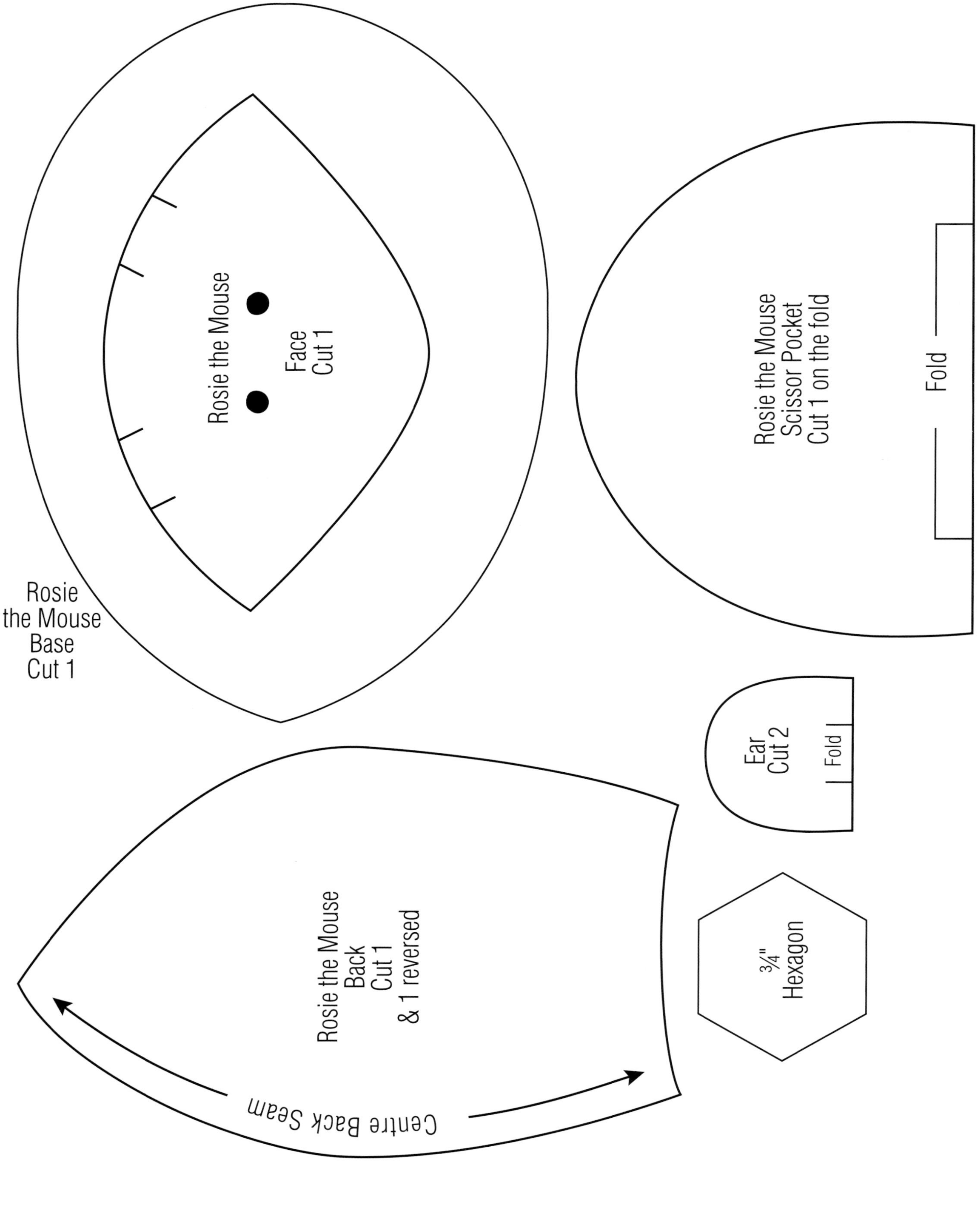

the Mouse Pincushion

Rosie the Mouse
Face
Cut 1

Rosie
the Mouse
Base
Cut 1

Rosie the Mouse
Scissor Pocket
Cut 1 on the fold

Fold

Rosie the Mouse
Back
Cut 1
& 1 reversed

Centre Back Seam

Ear
Cut 2

Fold

3/4"
Hexagon

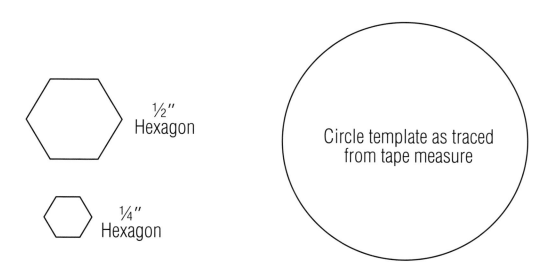

½″
Hexagon

¼″
Hexagon

Circle template as traced
from tape measure

Project on Page 134   With Love Liberty Gift Bag

*Heart Template

½″
Hexagon

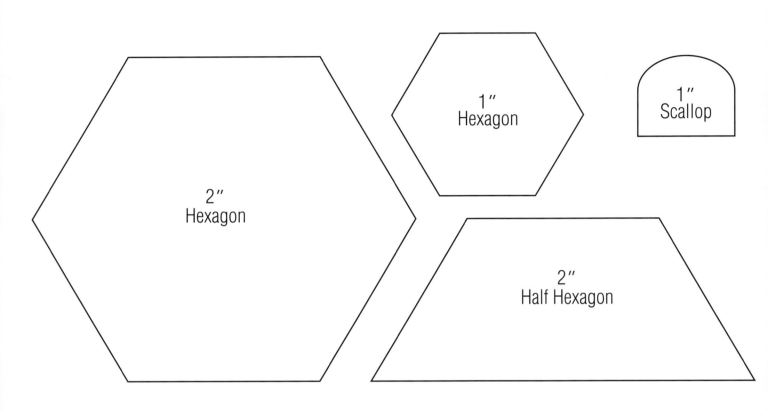

2" Hexagon

1" Hexagon

1" Scallop

2" Half Hexagon

Embroidery Design

*Pointed
Dresden

*Round
Dresden

Together
we make a
Family

Hand Quilting
Template

Flower
Embroidery

*Custom
Flower Petal

Butterfly Hand Quilting
Templates

*Custom
Heptagon

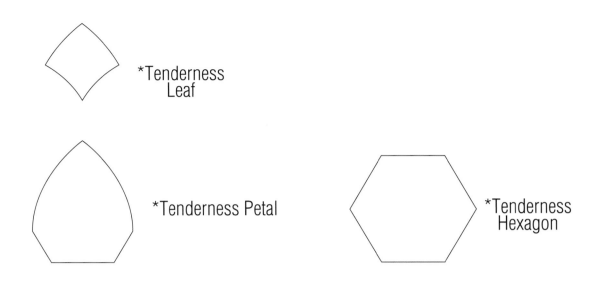

*Tenderness
Leaf

*Tenderness Petal

*Tenderness
Hexagon

*4" x 1.5" Rectangle

4" Square

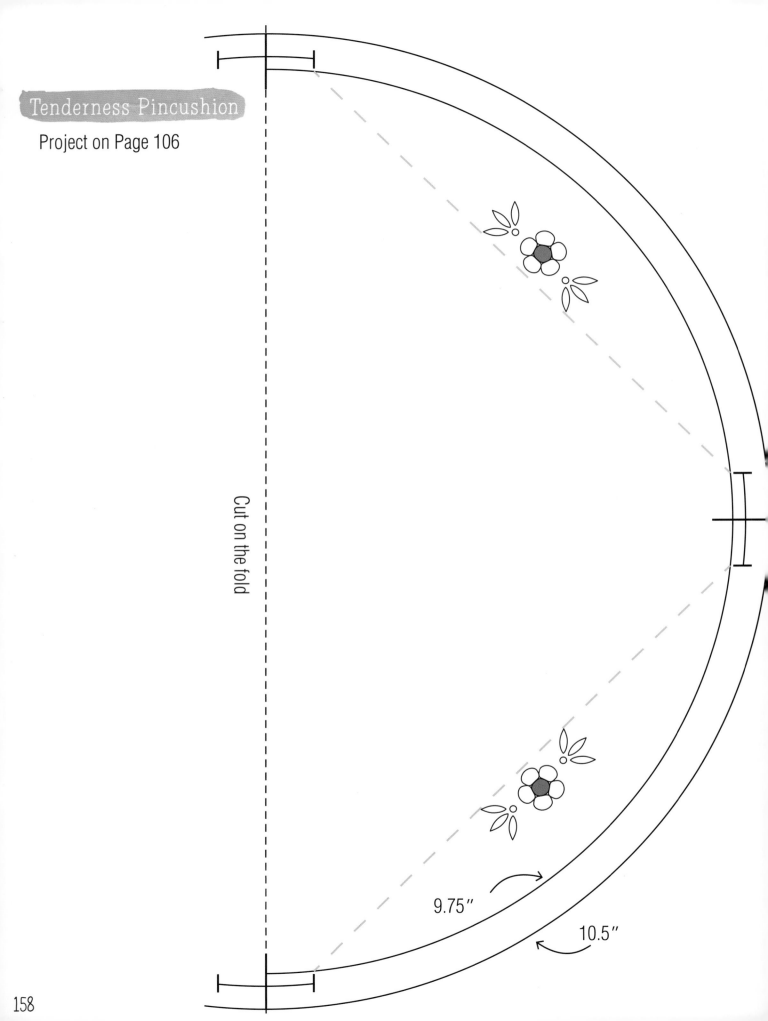

Tenderness Pincushion

Project on Page 106

Cut on the fold

9.75"

10.5"

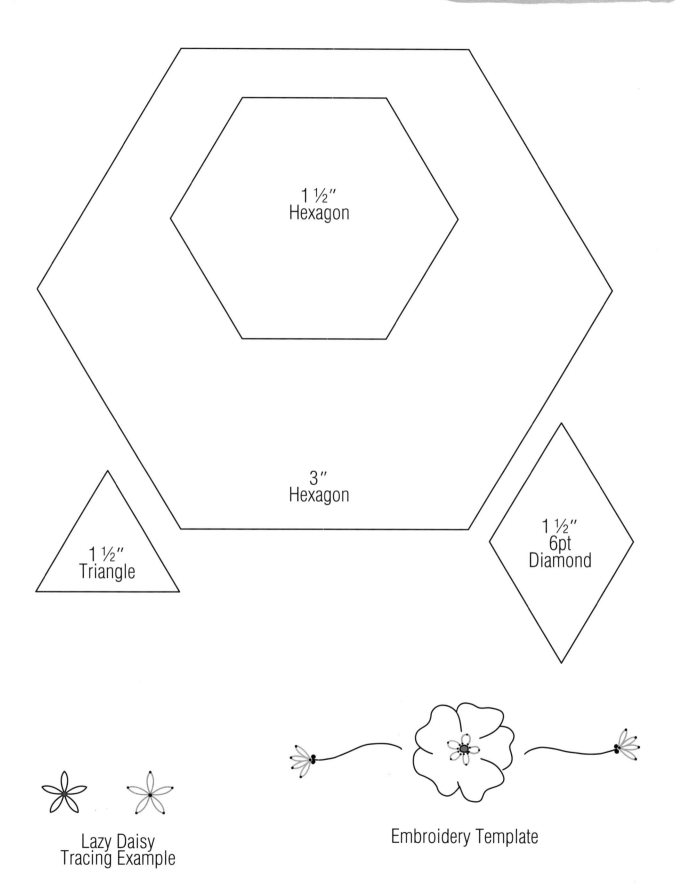

1 ½″
Hexagon

3″
Hexagon

1 ½″
Triangle

1 ½″
6pt
Diamond

Lazy Daisy
Tracing Example

Embroidery Template

Resources and Acknowledgements

There is something special about finding that perfect fabric for a new project.

Ava and Neve is a wonderful Australian shop full of Liberty Fabrics, supplies and notions. I would like to give a special thank you to Martina at Ava and Neve for the support of Liberty fabrics used within my book.
www.avaandneve.com.au

Thank You to Two Green Zebras here in Australia for the support of the Tilda fabrics used with in my book.

Two Green Zebras
sales@twogreenzebras.com
www.twogreenzebras.com

Tilda distributor United States of America - Devonstone Square
sales@devonstonesquare.com
www.devonstonesquare.com

To Julia and the team at Brother Australia, thank you for your continued support.

If you would like more information on the Sewing Machine that I use and my Scan N Cut, the CM900, please visit the links below.
www.brother.com.au/scanncut
www.brother.com.au/vq3000

A Special Thank You

To my family, thank you, you mean the world to me and without your support and unconditional love none of this would be possible.

To Glenn, thank you for the endless cups of coffee and the late-night chocolate runs. Thank you for turning my sketches into legible files, keeping me grounded and on task. For everything you do for me and our family, thank you a million times over. All my love xx

To my precious children, Lily, Keegan, Declyn and Aiden, please chase your dreams. Dream big and aim high, you never know what is possible until you try. Love Mum xx

To my Mum, thank you for letting me borrow your sewing machine all those years ago. It was just the beginning of an amazing journey. Love you xx